To:

_____

From:

_____

Date:

_____

The
WONDER
of
AMERICA

By
DERRIC JOHNSON

Honor Books
Tulsa, Oklahoma

The Wonder of America
ISBN 1-56292-628-4
Copyright © 1999 by Derric Johnson
P.O. Box 944
Sherwood, Oregon 97140

Published by Honor Books
P.O. Box 55388
Tulsa, Oklahoma 74155

Table of Contents

Dedication

I began celebrating the wonder of America while traveling abroad. I was directing The New Sounds, a folk group of college students from Skyline Wesleyan Church in San Diego, traveling through South America on a choir tour.

On July 4, 1965, we were singing in Medellin, Columbia. No one in that city cared anything about that special date, except for 500 Americans who worked for a variety of companies there. They gathered for a personal celebration, and The New Sounds provided the entertainment for the meeting. We closed the evening by joining hands in a giant circle and singing together "God Bless America." Standing there on the soil of a country not my own, sharing that powerful song about home, absolutely overwhelmed my mind and my heart. I never got over it.

To those patriotic pilgrims who began this journey with me, I lovingly dedicate this book. Thank you, New Sounds. You are still my valued friends and favored memories.

This book is lovingly dedicated to Sandi Barkman, Diane Beebe, Marilyn Blount, Mark Evans, Connie Fish, Dave Johnson, Chuck Joslyn, Carole Lofthus, Sheila Lorenz, Jan Martenson, Jerry Martenson, Rusty Phillips, Artie Price, Gail Romaine, Lari Schwab, Art Whaling, and Gary Wigdahl.

Introduction
The Wow! of America

A great subtitle for this book would be "Wow, I Didn't Know That!" Just wait and see how many times you say that before you finish this volume. It just seems to be the appropriate and universal response to the stories about fathers, footballs, farmers, Ferris wheels, and the many other facts that make up *The Wonder of America.*

These selections are gleaned from the radio show AMERICA IS, which aired on 750 stations daily, first throughout the bicentennial year and then many times since. Of the 366 shows (1976 was a leap year), here are 100 printed for your enjoyment and information. They transcend the celebrations of a bicentennial year, for they capture the best of America from and for every generation.

I didn't order these precisely, because I just went for the heart of America, which is (as it has always been) the people who live here, shaping her destiny and sharing her promise.

While history is all about dates and facts, these accounts are about people and truth. They are random stories with specific lessons, each one designed to warm your heart, touch your emotions, stimulate your mind, or tickle your funny bone. As you read, see how many times you say, "Wow, I didn't know that!"

Derric Johnson

Acknowledgments

Not many of us work well alone. Somehow things seem to go better when we're sharing. And maybe that's one of the strong lessons about the two-hundred-plus years of success that America is. George Washington had Ben Franklin and Tom Jefferson; there were two Wright brothers; and Abbot had his Costello!

Likewise there are many people who helped me create *The Wonder of America*.

Research and documentation, was done by the late Bob Benson Sr., who had the idea for this whole project in the first place; his son Robert Benson Jr., who chided us to correctness; and Robert Hempy, my longtime friend and ministry compadre who is the ultimate history buff.

Reassuring oohs and aahs came from my wonderful wife, Debbie—along with her endless editing, analysis, and encouragement.

Exactness and creativity are from the Editorial and Art Design team at Honor Books.

This book is one more example showing that cooperation is the key to success. Working with one another is still the best way to make things happen. Did you ever notice that freckles would make a great suntan if they could only get together!

Pepper by Sea

It was 1453 when the Turks conquered Constantinople and cut off the commerce between the East and West. In so doing, they deprived Europe of silks, jewels, and one other vital item, the spices of Asia. Thus, modern history, says Alistaire Cooke, began with the problem of how to bypass Turkey and get to the Spice Island of Indonesia by sea.

One man believed it could be done and that he was providentially chosen to do it. He was a six-foot, redheaded, fast-talking dreamer, filled with great quantities of curiosity, stubbornness, and sense of mission. A Christian of almost maniacal devoutness, he also longed for the secular trappings of pomp and power. He determined to convert every

prince and pauper in the Indies and have himself proclaimed governor of every land he discovered.

Finally after more than twenty years of searching for a royal sponsor, he set sail under the flag of Spain in three tiny ships with forty men. And on October 11, 1492, he sighted what he believed to be the mainland of Asia. In reality, it was San Salvador in the Bahamas.

To his dying day he never knew that he had not touched the Orient, or that he, Christopher Columbus, on a voyage to discover pepper by sea, had stumbled on the New World. Yet he possessed an unsinkable spirit that exemplifies the wonder of America!

The Horseplayer

There's an old saying that all horseplayers die broke. But as a matter of recorded fact, one of the heaviest players the American turf ever knew died rich, honored, and immortalized.

Like most horseplayers he had one eccentricity. Whenever there was a gray horse in the field, that was the horse he bet on. And when a horse from his own stable was running, he would bet on it to a point of monetary collapse. Oddly, for a man who died rich, he, more often than not, picked them wrong when he wagered. He made up for that with his shrewd horse-trading. For example, he once traded a valuable horse named Magnolia for 5,000 fertile acres in Kentucky. And would you believe, after that trade Magnolia never won another race?

So fierce was his passion for victory that, when the Stewards in Alexandria, Virginia, awarded winning honors to a rival entry in a close race, he advanced on them with such frenzied argument that he caused the Jockey Club to reverse the judge's decision and give the race to his horse!

However midway through his life, with extreme resolution, he turned his back on the excitement of the track, gave up his racing stables, and devoted himself to raising mules!

You can be glad, because from that venture he moved into the military, and eventually politics. And, that eccentric, passionate horseplayer became the Father of your country: George Washington.

Heat Was the Answer

Charles was one of those people who made a lot of money but never kept any. In fact he died $200,000 in debt—but he changed the whole world's idea of travel in doing so. The son of a New Haven, Connecticut, hardware merchant and manufacturer, Charles became a partner in the business in 1821 and watched it go bankrupt in 1830.

With the free time now available, he turned his attention to improving the quality of rubber. The rubber available then melted and decomposed in the summer or hardened and cracked in the winter. On borrowed capital, he began experiments that he continued in debtors' prison.

After hundreds of failures and on the edge of quitting, he

accidentally dropped some rubber on a hot stove; that was how he discovered that heat was the answer.

In 1844 he took out a patent for vulcanization but had to go to court to get it outright. The lawyer who helped him win his case was Daniel Webster. He received a $25,000 legal fee—much more than Charles ever realized for his effort.

To pay off his indebtedness, he sold his patent rights and gave the rubber industry to the world. Others may have made the money, but he made the product.

By the way, he did leave two things with his name on them—a company and a blimp—Charles Goodyear.

The Nut Tree

Halfway between San Francisco and Sacramento is the remarkable place called "The Nut Tree." In 1851 Josiah Allison went West to seek gold but instead found that the real treasure was in the soil and climate of California.

He brought his family from Iowa and settled down to plant and harvest. He set out fruit trees, and in 1860 he planted one black walnut beside the Emigrant Trail that passed his ranch.

That walnut that Josiah laid in the rich soil came to him as a gift from his twelve-year-old niece, Sally. On a hazardous journey to

California, angry Indians seriously injured Sally with an arrow. She and her mother wintered in Albuquerque. Then, when they were with a

wagon train in Arizona, she picked up the nut on the banks of the Gila River and brought it as her gift to Uncle Josiah in California.

The tree was cherished not only by the pioneer's family but also by every weary traveler who rested in its welcome shade. The ranch grew, and in 1921 a fruit stand was opened under Sally's giant tree.

Next came a restaurant, a toy shop, a miniature railroad, an airport, a shopping plaza, and a bake shop. Then in 1962 the United States Postal Service designated the area officially Nut Tree, California.

Today it's a million-dollar business—all because a little girl found a nut and gave it away.

Paper Patterns

Ebenezer lived in Sterling, Massachusetts, and made his living as a tailor of men's apparel. It was on a winter's night in 1863 that his wife was sitting at the dining room table trying to cut out a dress for their daughter. She became exasperated with the awkward task. "It would be a lot easier to do this if I had some kind of pattern to guide me," she fumed. Ebenezer had been quietly reading, but her comment interrupted his story.

Suddenly he was struck with a brilliant idea that revolutionized home sewing. Why not make sewing patterns out of paper? Until that

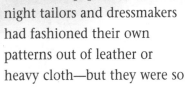

night tailors and dressmakers had fashioned their own patterns out of leather or heavy cloth—but they were so expensive that ordinary housewives couldn't begin to afford them.

Eb began to figure. He was sure that he could sell paper patterns for ten cents apiece and still make a profit. He shared his idea with other tailors, but they dismissed it as a "sheer waste of good time." Undaunted, he kept at it and in a few months was selling hundreds of patterns. Within a year he moved to New York and opened a sales office. Then he set up a factory to produce his patterns for national distribution, and soon he was selling six million patterns a year.

Every seamstress today will still recognize the name of the American tailor with a better idea—Ebenezer Butterick.

From Canvas to Code

Sam was an artist—one of the finest painters America ever produced. But that's not the reason there's a statue erected in his honor in New York's Central Park.

Sam was doing a portrait of the Marquis de Lafayette when he received a letter. He abandoned his portrait assignment and turned his back on his profession. He was no mechanic or scientist—let me say it again to underline it in your memory—Sam Morse was a great portrait painter. But he devoted the rest of his life to figuring out how to make electricity talk. He devised a system of dots and dashes which we know by his name—the Morse Code.

Why?

To understand why, you need to know what was in that letter in 1832.

It was a message that had come on horseback, and it had taken seven days for it to arrive. It simply said that Sam's wife was dead. Sam Morse was filled with the anguish of a man who felt that if he had been there it might have been different. At least if he had known that she was ill, he could have been with her until the end. So he committed himself to mass communication so no man must ever again learn—seven days late—that his wife had needed him.

The statue in the park is to the man who invented the telegraph. But the vast lacework of wire that wraps itself around us all is a monument to the woman he loved, Mrs. Sam Morse.

She died alone, and Western Union was born.

Little Pickett

One night in the middle of July, bonfires burned all along the Southern army's front lines. Across the line General U.S. Grant sent scouts to find out why. They reported that the fires burned in celebration of the birth of a son to Confederate General George Pickett.

Grant fingered his beard thoughtfully. Like Jackson and Lee and Sherman, he, too, belonged to that old brotherhood of the Mexican War, during which the then Second Lieutenant George Pickett, fresh from West Point, had recklessly planted the stars and stripes at the top of Chapultepec under heavy fire. Now Pickett had recently repeated this recklessness at the Pennsylvania town of Gettysburg by leading an

abortive advance in what was being called "Pickett's Charge."

The good news of Pickett's fatherhood spread through the Federal Camp that July night. They had all fought for the same thing once. "Well, let's strike a light for young Pickett ourselves," said Grant. And soon the bonfire salute ran the length of the Federal lines as well. A few days later a baby silver service, engraved to George Pickett Jr. was sent across the lines under a flag of truce from Pickett's former comrades-in-arms to his young son.

You see, even in war, they found some things were more important than fighting. Things like remembering, caring, and giving.

Can It

Gale was born on an upstate New York farm in 1801 and raised in Kentucky and Indiana by his roaming pioneer family. He had few opportunities for regular schooling, but he did learn surveying from his father. As a young man he easily earned his livelihood during his migrations through Mississippi and Texas.

In the 1830s he became involved as a strong activist in the movement for Texas' independence from Mexico. While he was in the Longhorn state, he became interested in the creation of concentrated food as provisions for wagon trains rolling west.

In 1842 he developed a meat biscuit, but his efforts to market it failed.

In 1851 he set himself up in a Shaker colony in New York, and there devised a method of evaporating milk in a vacuum for which he was granted a patent in 1856. Five years later he had secured the financing to establish a large condensory in Wassaic, New York. His evaporated milk, nourishing and easily carried, became available as rations for Union soldiers, and certainly it was a factor in keeping those troops healthy and on the road to victory.

He later returned to Texas and devised processes for concentrating various other foods, including cocoa and fruit juices. He kept perfecting his ideas and research. Gale's gift to us was a giant corporation that still bears his name: BORDEN'S.

The Problem and the Miracle

The year 1776 saw thirteen American colonies put together an army that ultimately defeated the forces of England. But the final battlefield victory was only a little more remarkable than the fact that the colonists were able to put together an army at all. Differences wider than geography separated the thirteen states that came together to form a more perfect union.

In Virginia and Maryland the nature of the land made large acreage farms possible, while from the Maine-New Hampshire border south to Pennsylvania, the basic unit was the one-family farm. This led to a great division in lifestyles. There were also strong differences between

those who lived in the sophisticated seacoast cities and those in the rural interiors.

Backgrounds varied a great deal also, from the Dutch of New York, to the Germans of Pennsylvania; from the Swedes of Delaware to the Scots of North Carolina. Then there were Quakers, Anglicans, Presbyterians, Puritans, and Catholics, all of whom knew little tolerance. Add to this decades of commitment to thirteen separate commonwealth colonies, some of which had originally fought one another, and you have the problem that led to the miracle.

Men from Maine and South united with men from Georgia and North under a general from Virginia to form one army, for one cause, for one nation: America.

The Other Rider

Did you know that a sixteen-year-old outrode Paul Revere? It's true! Young Ludington lived on a farm in New York with a father who was a captain of the state militia.

On the night of April 27, 1777, a messenger arrived on the Ludington farm with the urgent news that the British, in a surprise attack from Long Island, had burned the city of Danbury, Connecticut, and were advancing on the countryside. Every farmer must be called out immediately. Because the senior Ludington had to stay for military duty, the sixteen-year-old volunteered for the job of riding and calling the farmers to fight.

Grabbing a big stick, the young Ludington leaped on a horse and galloped off into the darkness. It was an all-night ride with pauses only long enough at each farm house to crash the stick against the door and shout a warning, "The British are coming! Get out and fight!"

And they did. Ludington mustered up enough men to not only stop the British—but also send them running back to their boats in defeat.

Ludington far outdid Paul Revere's famous ride. Paul only got about ten miles before the British at Lexington captured him. Ludington covered a staggering forty miles of hard riding.

It's interesting to note that one of America's first heroes was a sixteen-year-old girl named Sybil Ludington!

Named for a Horse

It was a long time ago in England when a sportsman went to the racetrack to win just one big one. He'd had a poor day and was down to the last race. He couldn't make up his mind on which horse to bet. So, his beautiful lady companion made up his mind for him. As a whim she placed a few pounds on a particularly handsome animal that struck her female fancy.

Of course it didn't matter to the lady that this beautiful horse had never won a race in his life. To her, he just looked good. In the language of the turf world however, he was just a plug. In any case, guided by her hunch, the English sportsman wagered all his money on that horse to win.

Well, as you can probably guess, the horse did win, and

paid a great deal of money. With this newly won fortune, the man journeyed to America, settled in California, and invested his entire riches in real estate. He prospered, and reinvested. His holdings mushroomed and became extensive. He kept buying and holding and buying some more.

Finally as a mark of honor, he named his immense real estate holdings after the English racehorse that made it all possible. For you see, from those holdings were born a community and a town that have become known and glamorized all over the world.

You'd never remember the name of the bettor, but I'll bet you'll never forget the name of his winning horse: HOLLYWOOD.

Pants for Sale

He was a Jewish immigrant from the Bavarian Alps in Germany. His parents were dead, he was bored with his job, and his brothers had gone to America. With no reason to stay, Strauss bought a one-way ticket to the land of his opportunity.

He was glad to meet his brothers in New York but surprised that they were not dressed in fine clothes and disappointed to learn that they were working as peddlers! But that was his opportunity, too, so Strauss spent three months learning the trade and enough English to realize that there was gold in California! He bought needles, threads, scissors, and thimbles, and a great quantity of heavy canvas from France, called denim, for making tents.

36

When Strauss got to San Francisco, he set up a display for his material. But the first miner to come by didn't want a tent, he wanted pants—with legs extra long so he could have patching material, and pockets extra tough so he could carry nuggets. So Strauss made denim pants instead of tents and sold out his first day! He opened a store and soon was marketing the strongest pants in the world.

That peddler became so much a part of the West that when he died his obituary was on the front page of the San Francisco newspaper. And 100 years after he left Germany, his company had expanded so that there was a warehouse there, distributing the pants with his name on them: LEVI'S.

Keep On

If at first you don't succeed, you're running about average. Out of the first four stores F. W. Woolworth opened, three failed. But, as you know, he kept at it. Admiral Perry attempted to reach the North Pole on seven different trips before he finally made it on the eighth. Thomas Edison tried 1,600 different materials before settling on carbon as the filament for the electric light bulb.

Oscar Hammerstein had five flop shows before OKLAHOMA! And then that ran for 2,248 performances. Similarly, Willie Mays didn't get a hit in his first twenty-six times at bat in the Major Leagues. Then on his twenty-seventh try he smashed a home run.

John Creasey's 560 novels sold more than sixty million

copies. But he collected 743 rejection slips from publishers before he managed to get one word in print. George Bernard Shaw was a bad speller, Benjamin Franklin a poor mathematician; Einstein was expelled from school for being mentally slow. And everybody knows Babe Ruth hit 714 home runs—but did you remember that he struck out almost twice that many times getting them?

You see. It's better to try to do something and fail than to try to do nothing and succeed. There are plenty of rules for attaining success, but somehow none of them work unless you work.

The Cross-eyed Dove

The next time you get to Nantucket, I want you to look at the gift shops. There's a special one I would like for you to notice. It's not the only gift shop in Nantucket, but it is the only one called "The Cross-eyed Dove."

You can't miss it.

It's owned and operated by a girl named Robin who used to work in someone else's store. All day long, she sold many things she didn't like to people she didn't know—people who were just passing through, going places she'd never heard of. Always in her heart, she knew she wanted her own place.

So one day she quit her job and borrowed some money, found an old house to fix up and began living out her dream. She wanted a shop that sold things she could believe in, things with texture and color and real value. She wanted things that could hold special meaning for special people. So, when you walk into her shop it's a little like walking into a warm, cozy living room on a winter's night, because Robin is that way. Now, the tourists don't pour in by the hundreds, but she does all right. She's not about to start a nationwide chain of gift shops called The Cross-eyed Dove, but she does want to move into a little better place someday.

I guess Robin's just like the rest of us, and what makes her special is what makes America special—the extra effort, the ability to dream, and the desire to make things better today than they ever were before.

The Victory Song

It's one of the oldest popular songs around, dating back to fifteen hundred. Farmers sang it in Holland. An English version poked fun at one of England's military leaders—Oliver Cromwell. The Italian words made light of the men's clothing style of the day.

When the British came to fight the Indians in the mid 1700s, the Colonists sent local forces to help. A professional British army surgeon took one look at the strange garb of the American forces and wrote a poem. The men from America seemed so untrained. He couldn't resist poking some fun. The words had a rhyme to them, and with a little experimenting, British regulars were able to put the new words to that same old tune.

But the Yanks liked it too. Americans, with a gift to laugh at themselves, started singing it, and soon the whole country was humming or whistling that simple tune. Then, when the Revolutionary War came, American soldiers made it their song by using it in camps, on the march, and before going into battle.

Written by the British as a joke, it became a song they regretted. One British General in the midst of the war said, "I hope I will never hear it again."

But they did! In particular, they heard it at Yorktown during the surrender of the British army to General Washington. And, as the Americans played that one song, "Yankee Doodle," over and over, a defeated enemy stacked their arms.

The Four Dollar Song

Before the Civil War our music was mostly hymns, minstrel songs, and the music of Europe. We didn't have many popular songs of our own. But in the war, music filled a common need. Old tunes were adopted as camp songs. One popular tune was the revival hymn, "Say Brothers, Will We Meet You Over on the Other Shore?" The soldiers had their own words for that one; "John Brown's Body" they called it.

Late in 1861, Union troops were singing their John Brown song as they marched through Washington toward the South. Julia Ward Howe saw that line of soldiers and heard the tune, and thought of some new words. She sent her poem to the *Atlantic Monthly*. It was published, and the editor sent her a check for $4.00.

An Ohio chaplain taught it to his regiment. They sang it as they marched off to war. Then others began to sing it, and the effect was magic. At a Washington rally attended by President Lincoln, it was sung. And with tears streaming down his cheeks, Lincoln exclaimed, "Sing it again."

We've been singing it ever since. That song was a real bargain for $4.00. You know it today as "The Battle Hymn of the Republic."

The Best Things

Eighteen hundred seven was a bad year for Americans. The new republic was tottering on infant legs. The British were shooting at us in a prelude to another war. And, economically, there was depression with prices soaring out of reach. But that bad year was also the year of the babies.

Nancy of Kentucky entered the valley of the shadow to bring a son, Abraham Lincoln, into the world. Wadsworth, America's great poet, was born that year, as was Cyrus McCormick, our noted inventor. It really wasn't a bad year when you look at the new babies.

And 1864 was an even worse year for America. Sherman was looting and burning American cities. Grant and Lee, old comrades in arms, were matching cruel weapons in Virginia. But Mary had her baby anyway in Diamond Grove, Missouri. That kind of a world needed a George Washington Carver.

We were at war with Mexico when tiny Tom Edison arrived and at war again when Edith gave birth to Charles in 1898. That's when our battleship Maine blew up, and the Spanish-American War with it. But it was a good year for the birth of someone who, one day, would heal others and found the Mayo Clinic.

So it's hard to be sure about bad years. Babies can turn our heads to a better future. Perhaps the best things happen at the worst times.

Yet to Be

I was standing on a wharf in New England. It was dark, and the fog had rolled in so thick that I could hardly see the lights of the sleeping village. A sign next to me said that if I traveled east by ship, the next light I would see should be Lisbon. All of America, as Thoreau once said, "was behind me."

On another day I stood on a cliff overlooking the crashing of the Pacific against the western edge of this land. And I knew that all of the Americas were still behind me. Then when I looked inland, I could see in my mind the people who started our country. Simple people, from

whose hard work a nation was fashioned from stone and wood and dreams. And I wished I'd been part of that America.

48

I saw the people coming west: the Boones, the Houstons, and the Fremonts. There they were—the settlers and adventurers whose courage and endurance had spanned a continent. And I wished I had been part of the America that was behind me.

Then I remembered John Kennedy. He said the American is a builder who builds best when called upon to build greatly. He spoke not only of the America behind us, but of the America before us. And looking inland from the fog-covered wharf in Nantucket to the cliffs overhanging the Pacific, I can see that all of America is not back there; it's out in front.

And I'm glad I'm part of the America that's yet to be.

Maps from Memory

Benjamin was born in 1731 near Baltimore, Maryland. Early in his life he showed great mechanical ability by taking his father's farm tools apart then reassembling them so they would work better. His grandmother taught him to read. His Quaker schoolmaster said he was an exceptionally bright pupil.

He was a wizard in mathematics, and he was a naturalist with great understanding about crops and weather. He even conducted one of the first studies of bees, and he completed mathematical research on the seventeen-year-locusts.

Benjamin made the first clock ever in America, even though he'd never seen one. Borrowing his mother's watch, working with only a small knife for tools, he took it apart, spread out the tiny wheels, and then reassembled it time and again. From this experience, he gained the idea for a chiming clock for which he carved all the parts from wood.

A neighbor taught Benjamin surveying and in 1790, the United States Government hired him for one of the most important jobs ever.

President Washington had appointed Major Lafant to draw up plans for a brand new city, but Major Lafant, in a fit of anger, packed up all the maps and plans and returned home to France.

We would have lost that city forever except for the memory of that brilliant black surveyor, Benjamin Baniger, who redrew all the maps from memory and gave us our Capitol—Washington, D.C.

Thanks to a Pigeon

The cornerstone was laid on July 4, 1848. It weighed 24,500 pounds, and it disappeared. No, I'm not kidding. Twenty thousand people witnessed the dedication of that tower and the installation of that block of marble. But somehow that 12-ton cornerstone got covered up and lost during construction, and to this day no one knows where it is.

But during the next 7 years the structure reached the height of 156 feet, and then work was suspended for 25 years.

In 1880 the Army Corps of Engineers was given the job of completing the hollow marble shaft. But the scaffolding and the ropes that ran to the top had rotted. Now remember, these were the days before

high-lift cranes and helicopters, so getting the new ropes up that high presented a problem. Anyway it did until the army engineers drafted a pigeon.

Inside the shaft, a thin wire was attached to the leg of the bird, and the noise of a gunshot sent it soaring, frightened, through the open top. Once outside, the bird landed. The wire that was attached to his leg was then used to haul up bigger ropes and finally a thick cable on which heavy scaffolding could be mounted.

Completed in 1884, the WASHINGTON MONUMENT stands today to its full height of 555 feet, thanks to a pigeon.

Music

Americans have an immense capacity for making music. It's something about the country's contrasts, its bustling cities, peaceful rivers, broad plains, and mountain peaks. Whether you go into a small town to hear the local high school band playing their yearly concert or enjoy a famed symphony, you find Americans making music.

We can make it at night in campsites with one guitar player or during great festivals of all kinds all across the country. We pipe it into our buildings, listen to it in our cars, and sing it to ourselves in the shower. Our love for music has given our country homegrown styles like country, bluegrass, gospel, jazz, and the blues. We sing fight

songs at athletic events and the National Anthem before them. We watch it on television and listen to it on our radios and record players. And it's common to find people singing to themselves as they rush back and forth at daily duties. It's kind of a national characteristic.

In Clay County, West Virginia, there's a man named John Harris. He lives back up in the mountains and makes guitars and banjos. He grew up around mountain music and learned to play it well. He will tell you that "music is all over this neighborhood. I couldn't have missed it if I tried!"

He's right, you know. Music is all around America. I don't think you could miss it if you tried!

Assistance of Heaven

Every Congressional session begins with a religious moment that is unique in the governing of modern nations. Activity pauses as the chaplain, chosen by Congress themselves, comes to the platform of the House to pray with and for the Legislators. Many times the piety and skill of the chaplain determine the effectiveness of that day's prayer. The impact of the singular message of each day's prayer is less important, however, than the unchanging power of the tradition of the moment.

It all began when that first Continental Congress met to establish a United States of America, and it has continued through the centuries as we struggle to preserve our nation. One day

the session was going badly. A lack of unity among representatives was threatening to break up the anticipated union of states.

Benjamin Franklin spoke up that day: "Mr. President, I have lived, sir, a long time. And the longer I live, the more convincing proof I see of this truth: that God governs in the affairs of men. And if a sparrow cannot fall to the ground without His notice, is it probable that an empire can rise without His aid? Except the Lord build a house, they labor in vain that build it. I therefore move that, henceforth, prayers imploring the assistance of Heaven be held in this assembly every morning."

It has been so ever since.

And so may it ever be.

The Great Benefactor

A ndy always said that wealth was a sacred trust to be administered for the public good. Not that anybody ever gave him anything, except opportunity; however, he appreciated that so much that he felt obligated to offer the same to as many people as possible.

You see. Andy was born the son of a weaver in Scotland. In 1848 his family immigrated to the New World and settled in Allegheny, Pennsylvania.

His first job was as a bobbin-boy in a cotton factory for $1.20 a week. Then he moved up to messenger and operator at Pittsburgh Telegraph office and from there to the Pennsylvania Railroad where he introduced the Pullman sleeping cars.

During the Civil War he organized the Union Army telegraphic service and foresaw expansion of railroads along with the growth of heavy industry after the conflict. And that growth would give rise to a great demand for iron and steel.

In 1865 he opened the Keystone Bridge Co. Within ten years it was producing one-fourth of our nation's steel. In 1901 a conglomerate called U. S. Steel was formed to buy him out.

Andy retired to philanthropy. Because he loved books and believed in culture and knowledge, he gave to libraries and institutions of higher learning $350,000,000.

He was one of America's great benefactors: Andrew Carnegie.

One Man's Problem

A twenty-six-year-old Yankee clockmaker in Concord, New Hampshire, believed in getting to work on time. To do so, he needed to arise at four in the morning. The sun was far from shining at that hour, so Levi Hutchins often overslept.

And that bothered his conscience so much that he began to think of a clock that could sound an alarm at a predetermined hour. He developed a mechanism that used the hour hand to trip a pinion that in turn sounded an alarm bell. He placed it within a pine cabinet 14" x 29" in dimensions.

The year was 1787. The first alarm clock had been designed: the granddaddy of the bells, buzzers, and soft music awakeners

of today. Hutchins wrote of this first model: "It made sufficient noise to awaken me almost instantly."

In his lifetime, the alarm clock was mass-produced internationally, and Hutchins saw thousands of his countrymen find new punctuality through his invention. What, you may wonder, sort of great fortune did Hutchins make through this timepiece breakthrough?

None!

He never patented his invention; he just wanted to wake up on time. Levi Hutchins lived to the age of ninety-four, and when asked what reward his invention had brought him, he replied, "I was never late again!"

No Place Like Home

It's rare when people make it bigger in the theater than John Howard Payne. He was a boy prodigy, publishing his own work at fifteen, becoming a successful actor at eighteen, and at twenty-two, gaining fame that earned him an engagement on the London stage.

At that time, the early nineteenth century, Europe was the theatrical center of the world. So for the next twenty years, John Payne remained in London, acting and writing. Finally, he returned to America, but the stay was a brief one.

Then President of the United States, John Tyler, appointed him as the American consul at Tunis, Africa. It was a highly honored post, but at the same time a lonely place. After serving another twenty years away from America, Payne died there in Africa. His last request was that his remains be brought home. This was done with great national attention, but not for his fame as an actor or his success as an ambassador.

John Howard Payne was being honored for a song he wrote, just one song. A song composed by this man who lived forty years away from the place he loved.

We remember him today for the words, "Be it ever so humble, there's no place like home."

The Man Who Wouldn't Quit

An ambitious Ohio businessman gained an appointment for his son Sam to attend West Point. It was a chance for a strange boy who loved only horses to find an education and a career. But his record at West Point was riddled with demerits for sloppy dress and tardy drills.

Oh, the Mexican War rescued Sam for awhile with a bit of glory. But then during bleak barracks duty in Oregon, far away from family, Sam drifted to discouragement and eventually despair. His commanding officer, finding him drinking while on duty, offered him the choice of a court martial or resignation.

Sam chose the latter.

With a growing family, he turned to business; he failed.

He tried farming; he failed there, too. In 1859 he sold firewood for a living, and he was reduced to a poverty level of existence. At forty, life had passed him by. But he didn't give up. He knew his moment would come, and when it did, he would be ready. He was.

In two years, the war that had been a long time coming arrived, and the country turned for leadership to a former failure who somehow never learned to quit. In four short years the same man who had been selling wood by the roadside became commander of all American armies on the field, and in nine years he became President of the United States.

Ulysses S. Grant was the man who wouldn't give up.

He Gave Himself a Name

"It's a crime equal to treason!" declared one newspaper. President Theodore Roosevelt had entertained a black man at dinner in the White House, something that had never been done before!

The object of the furor was a forty-five-year-old, mild-mannered gentleman who had been a slave until the age of nine. As a boy, he'd worked in a salt furnace beginning at 4:00 A.M. so he might get to school for the morning classes. That's why he said the classroom was the same as getting into Paradise.

In 1881 he was asked to take charge of what was to be a school for black students. It wasn't much to begin with, a few broken-down buildings, at best. But he would often say, "I want to see education as common as grass, and as free for all as the sunshine and rain."

You know what? He made it that way for the black community of Alabama.

When he died thirty-four years later, he had created an institution which owned 30,000 acres of land and 100 buildings, possessed an endowment of two million dollars, and was teaching thirty-eight trades and professions.

Not bad for a former slave whose first home had a dirt floor, whose first shoes were made of wood, and who, in his first classroom experience, was asked for his surname, and because he didn't have one, gave it to himself—Washington.

I'd like you to meet Booker T. Washington of the now renowned Tuskegee Institute.

The Vulgar Book

The new book was called vulgar and barbarous. Critics mocked the work in both the United States and England.

The author was ambitious, vain, and intensely patriotic. He felt that America must be as independent in literature as she was in politics.

His highly criticized book was not written lightly or carelessly. He studied twenty-six languages in preparation for his literary masterpiece. He traveled widely through all the American states, listening to what people said and how they said it. He made notes of all he heard, speaking with frontiersmen as well as cultured businessmen.

He gave a total of twenty-eight years to the preparation

and writing of this one book. His authorly ideals were high, for he expected this one book to forge the America of the early nineteenth century into one committed body of citizens. He really expected that his one work might forever bind Americans to one another inseparably.

When the book was published in 1828 and met with initial hostility and criticism, in no way was the author dissuaded from his big dreams for the book.

His dream was right. His book did famously link us to each other.

Millions of copies have been printed. Lexicographer Noah Webster wrote *An American Dictionary of English Language,* and his vulgar book made it big.

It Touched the Sky

She was only twenty-five, but the pressures of life had already etched old lines on her girlish countenance. She had watched and waited for her soldier husband, but he never returned. All that came was that letter from his commanding officer: "Killed in battle."

So, every day became the same: her hands moving to and fro, weaving lace; her mind moving back and forth, counting the dark things fate can do. But one day was different; light broke through her shadowed life. A light

brought by a commanding figure who asked for help, help not just for himself— General George Washington— but for his struggling new nation, America.

That shining light caught her soul.

Together they drew and shaped and planned and wove and worked—six white bands and seven red bars with a corner of blue to lay some stars. General George suggested stars with six points, but the seamstress was adamant—no six-pointed star on her flag! Those were British stars, and to them she'd lost her husband. Only five points would do. They were symbols of freedom. She had her way.

Betsy Ross began to manufacture large numbers of flags for the colonies. And, as she worked, the light that began in her small sewing room flared to the world as it touched the sky.

The First Hero

He'd been teaching school for two years when the war began. He was only twenty-one, a little above average height, with fair skin, blue eyes, and light hair. And, he was involved in the Long Island campaign that was just this side of disastrous. We were facing the enemy across the East River not knowing what their plans might be. Fearing surprise more than anything, General Washington wanted someone to sneak over the lines and get information.

Spying is a dirty job, and nobody wanted it; so Nate volunteered. There is something about taking on a job that's got to be done that's the custom of American heroes. Dressed like a Dutch schoolmaster, he ventured through the enemy lines. He got what he went after and was on his way back when the British found the information on him. He admitted he was a spy, and they hanged him the next morning.

Before he died, he wrote a few letters home, but the British destroyed them so that "the rebels should not know they have a man who can die so firmly." In his last moment though, they let him say what he wanted to.

He was just a young American who had no time to do anything memorable but die. So he stood there with the noose around his neck and told them his rank, Captain, his name, Nathan Hale, and then he added:

"I only regret that I have but one life to lose for my country."

In so doing he showed the world what Americans are made of.

A Handshake Away

America is only a little over 200 years old, just two centuries! The Boston Tea Party, Bunker Hill, George Washington, they all seem to be relics of a dim and distant past. The lovely trees and well-kept markers serve only to make the epochs of the past seem long ago and far away. Anything 200 years old seems ancient!

I mean Uncle Sam ought to have white hair and whiskers! But the posters with his picture have it wrong.

Uncle Sam is a young man! My grandfather, whose hand I touched, could shake the hand of a man who shook the hand of another man who shook hands with George Washington! I'm just

three handshakes away from Washington, Jefferson, Franklin, and all the founding fathers of our country.

We're not an old, old nation. Not really. America is just a young upstart, beginning to flex her muscles. Imagine, if you will, our serving as mediators in a war between 2 nations more than 5,000 years old, both of them more than 25 times as old as we are?

No, don't let the 200 fool you. You don't live in an old country whose story is nearly all told. We are a young land, and a young people whose great contributions and ideas are yet to come. And they will grow out of the dreams and hopes we have and will contribute.

So next time you notice a new gray hair or get a humorous birthday card emphasizing your advancing years, just remember you are part of the world's youth movement and only a couple of handshakes away from our founding fathers!

Courage by Candlelight

You think women of the Revolutionary War period were purely Victorian—patient, long-suffering, and passive—don't you? Well, those American women had a fierce streak of independence and a capacity for great courage unlike anything ever seen before: courage by candlelight.

Take, for example, the time one Pennsylvania woman named Deborah braved an angry mob in Philadelphia. She picked up a gun when she and her home were threatened and sent that mob packing. If they hadn't, she would have used that gun. Deborah was some woman.

What about Abigail? She wrote often to her patriot husband, giving him ideas for speeches and suggestions for

practical philosophy of independence. By her own husband's admission, Abigail drove him into American leadership.

She once wrote to him: "Difficult as the day is, I would not exchange my country for the wealth of the Indies." Well said, Abigail.

Betsy was younger when the war came. Her marriage came right in the midst of the conflict. In fact, her husband was a colonel in Washington's artillery who was destined to become a member of the President's Cabinet. And Betsy was with him through it all.

Without these women, and others like them, there could hardly have been any founding fathers. Women like Mrs. Benjamin (Deborah) Franklin, Mrs. John (Abigail) Adams, and Mrs. Alexander (Betsy) Hamilton.

They are courage by candlelight.

It Couldn't Be Done

Bishop Milton Wright handled his western jurisdiction of the United Brethren Church with the skill he'd learned over a half century of churchmanship. His area was the sprawling, growing West of these United States just at the turn of the century. Of the many pronouncements he was called on to make, one was a judgment on several popular writings of the day suggesting that man might design and construct a machine that would make him airborne. A statement by Bishop Wright was obviously needed.

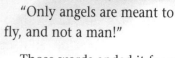

"Only angels are meant to fly, and not a man!"

Those words ended it for all loyal churchmen. But it was near this same time that two

young men, two brothers in their thirties, labored on a primitive machine at the sandy beach of Kitty Hawk, North Carolina. These brothers had a great faith to add to the very doubtful project. You see. They believed that it could be done.

Men, as well as angels, should fly.

Their first attempts were abortive. They didn't even get off the ground. But finally, on a lonely beach, the brothers proved Milton Wright wrong when their flying machine became airborne for a total of 128 feet.

And what were their names?

Orville and Wilbur Wright, of course, the famous sons of Bishop Milton Wright, who once said it couldn't be done.

Spectacular Monument

The Chicago Exposition had to have some spectacular monument, and a thirty-four-year-old American bridge builder named George had an idea. But some of the nation's leading engineers insisted his dream was preposterous and unsafe. So George had to convince them, one by one, of his technical knowledge.

Everyone knew that a bridge with that much steel would require a year to build, and this much more complex structure George had in mind must be completed in just four and one-half months.

"Impossible," they said.

Yet, his "impossible" dream was completed on the eve of the Fair. Then the skeptics were at it again when it was announced that he would be unable to attend the dedication. Sick? Who could believe that? Well, his wife did. And public confidence was glued together again when she went up first, making the ascension to the top of that "thing" which was taller than a twenty-five-story building.

When she came down, thousands went up. And the tower George built never did pass from the American skyline. But, he never knew. You see. He really was ill that day.

Tuberculosis.

He died a few weeks later. But his contribution to the Chicago Fair has replicas everywhere today, keeping his name alive in gaily-colored lights around the world.

The bridge builder of 1893 was George Washington Gale Ferris. And his monument is the Ferris wheel.

Careful, It's Hot

The World's Fair of Chicago in 1893 was maybe the greatest ever. There were two men named George who helped draw the crowds with startling new attractions: George Ferris, with his famous wheel, and George Westinghouse who went over the head and influence of Thomas Edison to light the whole park with his brand of electricity—alternating current.

Most of us have been so taken with those big accomplishments that we've almost forgotten that Anton was there too. And when you get right down to it, Anton did as much as either of the two famous George's.

He had come to America from Bavaria with a favorite recipe and was trying to sell his specialty at the Fair. The one problem was that his food had to be served steaming hot; and that made it difficult for fair-goers to handle, so most of them passed it up for more conventional nourishment.

Anton even tried providing white gloves to protect the hands of his customers, but somehow the gloves kept walking off with the people, and that got expensive.

Just before he gave it all up, Anton got an idea. Why not protect his customers' burning fingers by putting his specialty between the halves of a long roll.

From that moment on he was a success, and the little sausage he served became known throughout the world as the American hot dog.

One Man's Fight

Every midshipman at the Annapolis Naval Academy sees many times the words inscribed in the Chapel, "I have not yet begun to fight." These words have become a part of American folklore. They bring to mind that certain September day in 1779 when Captain John Paul Jones engaged and defeated a new British warship off the coast of England.

Most of us picture a confident captain uttering these words on the deck of a sturdy American warship with the enemy soon to sink in defeat. The facts, however, are far different.

Jones' ship, the Bonhomme Richard, was a rotting fourteen-year-old, purchased by our new government from the harsh Indian trade game. His cannons were secondhand, and several of them exploded at the first volley.

The battle brought seven feet of water into his hold because of a mistaken broadside given by a sister ship. And what of his words, "I have not yet begun to fight."? Well, they were actually shouted at his men at their guns.

Finally, when His Majesty's ship the *Serapis* struck her colors in surrender, the prisoners outnumbered the victors, and the Bonhomme Richard was the sinking ship, barely kept afloat long enough to receive the surrender.

So, if the truths are known, America's first naval victory was really a one-man affair.

Pilgrims

A few years after James became king, a number of the Separatists living in the village of Scrooby, England, made up their minds to form a church of their own. They met for worship every week in the home of William Brewster, one of their members. The king was displeased.

"Since these men do not obey me," he declared, "they must be punished."

And they were. A few were thrown into prison; some were hanged. But the Separatists believed they were right. They decided to leave their country and venture to Holland where they could worship God as they pleased.

They first traveled to Amsterdam, then they settled in Leydon. They were still unhappy. They didn't want their English children using Dutch ways and words. They simply wanted a new country where they could have religious freedom and still train their children to be English in language, manners, and habits.

King James was unwilling for them to live anywhere under his rule, but finally agreed to not disturb them in America, if they gave him no trouble. So they borrowed money and sailed from Holland to England. There, they hired a small ship called the Mayflower and sailed from London. After sixty-four days at sea, they anchored off the New England coast.

Because of their wanderings, they called themselves Pilgrims. And it's important to remember that men first crossed the Atlantic not to find soil for their plows, but to secure liberty for their souls.

Trade for Life

One night in 1865 a band of Missouri night raiders kidnapped a mother and her young son. They wanted to sell them as slaves, and it didn't seem to bother anybody. Anybody, that is, except a kindly farmer who set out in pursuit of those nightriders to rescue that little boy and his mother.

After days of searching, the farmer located the kidnappers. The mother had vanished, but they still had the boy. The farmer pleaded for the life of that sick little lad and finally struck a bargain with the kidnappers. He agreed to pay a ransom; he gave a $300 racehorse in exchange for the boy's freedom. The swap was made: a human life for a horse.

In time, the ailing boy recovered and grew up, and

countless millions of people were blessed by his living. He became one of America's greatest scientists. His many important discoveries affected the lives of people everywhere.

He introduced the soybean to America. He developed and popularized the peanut of the South so that crop became a valuable source of cheese, beverage, washing powder, ink, and synthetic rubber. He pioneered the use and understanding of dehydrated foods. His discoveries saved billions of dollars and made millions of lives happier.

The boy who was traded for a horse grew into the beloved scientific benefactor, Dr. George Washington Carver.

The Famous Farmer

American agricultural know-how began with one man, a farmer in Virginia who was the first man in the New World to rotate his crops. He first planted tobacco and wheat: the next year, buckwheat that he plowed under. Then wheat again. And after three years he put the land back in grass and clover. Then he tried corn and potatoes. His harvest of wheat multiplied twenty-five times in five years.

Then for the first time in America, wheat was planted in drilled rows. He did it with an invention of his own. And he was constantly experimenting with all kinds of natural fertilizer and compost.

He continually fought against erosion, as time after time he dragged mud back to the ridge-land from where it had washed away. Still to this day, the soil he nourished produces crops. Trees still stand that were planted by his hand.

Of all the honors that came his way, of all the titles that adorned his name, none filled him with pride more than the wheat-spikes that he had added to his family coat of arms. It did so because those spikes of wheat proclaimed to all who saw them that he was a farmer.

The man who invented the seed drill and pioneered scientific fertilization and crop rotation, the gentleman farmer of America who established the first experimental farm's history, is remembered mostly for what he considered lesser things. For no matter what his accomplishments on the stage of the nation, George Washington always remained, at heart, a farmer.

For the Birds

John's father wanted him to be a sailor; John just wanted to watch birds build nests, feed their young, or perch on a limb to sing. He spent hours roaming the countryside and filled the rooms of his house with drawings of Phoebes, Peewits, Orioles, and Cardinals.

But when he met Lucy his father said, "You've got to get into business. You can't support a wife by drawing pictures of birds."

So, John started merchandising in Kentucky. It was winter when he arrived and only a few birds were around, so John stuck to the business, made some money, and married Lucy.

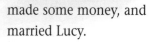

But when spring came, he'd leave the store, sometimes for

days, wading through marshes, swimming the river, roaming wherever birdcalls could be heard. In short order the business failed and John was jailed. Finally his creditors settled the debts by taking everything John had, except his bird pictures which they considered worthless.

Lucy encouraged him to keep drawing, and in 1837 his pictures titled *Birds of America* were published. Some people call him a scientist because his pictures are so exact; and because he depicted so many species, he's called an ornithologist.

But most of all he's remembered, because the people who watch birds today call their society by his name, John James Audubon.

Lee's Garden

The beautiful land rolls up from the Potomac River on the Virginia side. Originally part of the estate of George Washington, the tract passed to his adopted son, George Washington Parke Custis, whose daughter Mary Ann Custis married Robert E. Lee.

The Lees lived almost twenty years in the beautiful home where they could stand on the porch and look at the Capitol in Washington, D.C., just across the river.

Although Robert E. Lee became the living symbol of the Confederate cause, he was

actually locked in a battle he never sought. He had freed his few slaves long before the war began and was opposed to secession.

He was offered the command of all Union forces, but his ancestors' long association with Virginia caused him to cast his lot with the South. With his family, he moved deeper into Virginia and never lived again in the beautiful hilltop mansion. And three years into the Civil War, the Federal Government seized the entire 1100-acre estate for nonpayment of taxes, a sum total of $98.16.

They buried Union soldiers in Mrs. Lee's rose garden and built a fort and a hospital on other parts of the land. Today, you will find 60,000 graves on this land including two Presidents and the tomb of the Unknown Soldier.

We now call Robert E. Lee's beautiful land Arlington National Cemetery.

A Man of Stone

Wars have a way of making men, or at least revealing what's in them—like this one. It was the first full-blown conflict of the Civil War. Southern troops were wavering, except for one brigade that stood like a wall of stone. It was under the command of Thomas J. Jackson, and the name Stonewall was born.

For the next two years his army moved so fast that it became known as the Foot Cavalry. In one thirty-eight-day period his men marched 400 miles, fought three major battles, plus a number of smaller ones, and won them all. In  doing so, they caused Northern authorities to use six armies to protect themselves from this lone band of mostly barefoot men.

A strangely private, devotedly Christian man, Stonewall Jackson never smoked or drank, never revealed his battle plans to anyone, and would not read a letter or plan a battle on Sunday. He gave God the credit for every victory, and believed the only safe military order was "Advance!"

Where did we get such a man? It seems, from the edge of nowhere. He'd been a slow learner at West Point where he was remembered mostly for his strange stubbornness. He became a Math instructor at Virginia Military Institute, and then, the War. With it, there was revealed the man of stone.

How many today can rise to the challenge of this hour?

A.C. O.K.

We'd been experimenting for some time with electricity. Even Thomas Edison said it couldn't be done, and he nearly succeeded in pulling the switch on George's idea. George had an idea for a new thing called alternating current that could be transmitted over wires for miles.

He developed transformers and set up an experimental power station in Pittsburgh. But when a small boy was accidentally electrocuted by one of George's wires, an anti campaign started. Ordinances were passed forbidding the stringing of high tension wires in many cities.

And that's when Edison wrote: "There is no plea which will justify the use of alternating current."

But George kept on. He went to Chicago and bid on a contract to light the World's Fair in 1893. He succeeded, in large part because his bid was so low.

Then he had to invent the manufacture to produce enough light bulbs to do the job. He lost a fortune but won public support. A few months later Niagara Falls was harnessed to turn generators to supply alternating current, and you know the rest.

George kept inventing. He took out patents at the rate of one every ninety days, and they gave rise to sixty companies and four new industries. But his biggest triumph was the one over Edison.

And, we need to thank George Westinghouse for American alternating current. A.C. is O.K.

The Eagle

Scarcely had the ink dried on the signatures of the Declaration of Independence that the Continental Congress appointed Benjamin Franklin, John Adams, and Thomas Jefferson as a committee of three to choose an appropriate symbol to go on the great seal of our new nation. But it took until 1782 for an appropriate symbol to be agreed upon, accepted, and approved by Congress. Only then was it finally placed on that seal.

It was to be the great American eagle. The first American pennies bore the eagle, as did our first

American flag. During the Civil War a live eagle named Old Abe was carried into battle perched on top of the staff of a shield.

However, the Americans were not the first to turn to the eagle as a national symbol. Caesar's legions marched under the Imperial eagle; so did Prussia's rulers, as well as the Czar of Russia. But America chose its eagle for a special reason.

In one talon the bird holds an olive branch of peace, and in the other a bundle of arrows, symbolizing preparedness for war. On the breast there is an unsupported shield, showing America's need to rely on her own resources. As inspirational as these may be, perhaps the noblest part of our national symbol is the most obvious.

The eagle is to be free—free to soar to the heights, to move, to change. The American eagle was never meant for a cage but always for the sky.

Footprints

There's a stone mason in Ohio named Carl Bates. Carl says that he can't imagine doing something all your life where you go home and maybe a year later you can't even tell what you've done. That's why he likes his work. He remembers the first blocks he ever laid forty years ago. And he never passes that house without thinking about it.

In New York City, Tom Patrick is a fireman. He's thirty-two, married, and he works very hard. He likes being a fireman because it gives him something to point to. He says, "It's real. It's what I want to be. I can point to a fire I put out. I helped somebody. It shows I did something on this earth."

Billie Cabbs lives in a little town in Alaska that doesn't

even have a road. You have to travel seventeen miles across the bay just to get there. If you ask Billie why she stays, she'll tell you, "Because here in this town I can leave a footprint. We all want that, don't we?"

America is a land of dreams, because it's a land of people who dream of doing something they can point to. Stone masons, firemen, people in big cities, people who live in isolated places, ordinary people—all 210 million of them. America! An extraordinary land made from extraordinary dreams of ordinary people.

One Thing in Common

They are, at best, a strange group of men. Yet one unique bond ties them to each other for as long as America records her history.

One was a poor Irish immigrant who died prematurely, leaving a sister to raise his three young sons.

One was so Dutch that English was not spoken in the home.

Another was a Scotch-Irish farmer who never quite made it big, except in children (he fathered nine).

Two were preachers of small churches.

One was a self-appointed doctor; he never earned a legitimate medical degree, but took a course by correspondence and then went from farm to farm offering his questionable services.

Still another, a poor laborer, never lived to see the birth of his youngest son.

Iowa was the state of another; he was a blacksmith.

Tavern-keeper, frontiersman, itinerant salesman, tanner of hides, mule-trader, trolley-car conductor, none really made a mark in a grand and great way.

All mostly ordinary men in what could be called, at best, small professions. Yet each of these men made it big in one way, and it is this that binds these men of two centuries into one special class.

Each one had a son who became a President of the United States.

Two Boys from Kentucky

Two babies were born a year apart in Kentucky. Both were boys, one in Christian County, and the other in Hardin. All of it was frontier then, Daniel Boone country with all the trimmings of the raw wilderness.

One boy's family moved north, hoping for better farming opportunities. The other boy remained in Kentucky.

One young man went to West Point and entered military service while the other became a small town clerk and postmaster. History shows that these were but temporary tasks for both.

Eventually, the two boys from Kentucky found themselves sharing the same profession: politics. One went from the U.S. Congress to the Senate to the

Cabinet of a President. The other also served in Congress as well as a state legislature.

And, when the country split in Civil War they split with it. The boy from Hardin County went with the North, the one from Christian County to the South. Then, in a strange quirk of fate, the year 1861 found these two, though far apart in philosophy, separated by just a few miles. For you see, one lived in Washington, D.C., and the other made his home in nearby Richmond, Virginia. And so they would live for the next four long years of war.

These two young boys from neighboring counties in Kentucky rose to become presidents: Jefferson Davis, President of the Confederacy of America and Abraham Lincoln, President of the United States.

Imagine, just two boys from Kentucky.

Molly Pitcher

A gift of cold water is often the best gift of all. Especially when thirst is real, and the heat is fierce. And that's how it was that hot summer day in 1778 near Monmouth Courthouse in New Jersey.

The temperature rose to 96 degrees as American and British soldiers were locked in terrible conflict; the constant firing of cannon and musket made it pass the 100-degree mark. Men on both sides dropped in their tracks, not from their wounds, but from the heat.

John Hayes, an American artillery sergeant, overcome by the heat of that torrid day, fell, and there was no one to replace him. But his wife Molly Hayes was there. She had followed her husband

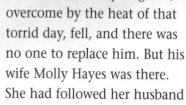

from camp to camp throughout the war. She immediately jumped in to take his place, swabbing, loading, and firing the cannon. But it was the heat and thirst of the men that really gripped her heart. Water became more important to Molly than cannon fire.

She began to carry great pitchers of water to wounded men whose suffering was terrible. She did this for her fellow Americans and for an enemy who was just as thirsty. You've seen Molly Hayes in battleground paintings from the Revolutionary War, standing there with cannon swabber in hand, and a bandage on her face. But the real legacy of Molly came from the men of both armies.

They gave her a name. Not for her gunnery skill but for the water she carried to them. They dubbed her Molly Pitcher.

The Other Big Day

July 4, 1776! That's the big American day—the date that a Declaration of Independence was adopted, and because of it, names like Jefferson and Hancock are easily remembered.

But, what about farmer Caesar Rodney and July 2, 1776, you ask?

That was the day when the Continental Congress met to try to break a deadlock in voting. The day before, July the first, a preliminary vote to break with the mother country showed nine colonies in favor, two opposed, one abstaining, and one deadlocked.

By July second, the two opponents had come over for independence, as had the abstainer. That left one remaining questionable state,

Delaware—a very important vote, if you will.
For, the members of congress believed that
unanimous approval was essential to break
something as important as a 169-year-old
political tie.

Thus, on July second, Delaware's third delegate,
Caesar Rodney, after an all-night ride, entered the
State House on Walnut Street in Philadelphia.

"The thunder and rain delayed me" he
explained, matter-of-factly. Then he reported
Delaware's support for independence.

Though it was years in coming, independence
was settled that day. Thirteen states declared
they ought to be free and independent.

July fourth was then inevitable. And, it had
to happen, just as it did, because of July second
and a farmer named Caesar Rodney.

Remember Sarah

In 1621, famous Pilgrim William Bradford proclaimed a day of feasting to commemorate the first harvest after a long year of suffering. That became America's first Thanksgiving Day.

But as the colonies grew more prosperous, the people forgot all about Thanksgiving and the meaning it held for their ancestors. The holiday was revived for a time under George Washington, but general interest in it dropped steadily. Finally it was observed in only a few communities, and that was sporadic and with no set date.

Then a determined woman named Sarah Hale appeared on the scene. She was a young widow from New Hampshire who in 1822 found herself with five children to support. She turned to

literature and became the editor of a women's magazine. Like most editors, Sarah was a crusader, and it was her belief that the government should make Thanksgiving a national holiday. She pounded away at her idea for years. Three Presidents turned her down. But the fourth finally agreed with her, and in 1863 Abraham Lincoln proclaimed the last Thursday of every November as our national day of Thanksgiving.

You probably never knew that Sarah Hale did that for you. Her fame rests more on a ditty that she wrote in 1830. None of us will ever forget that simple poem that starts . . .

Mary had a little lamb,

Its fleece was white as snow.

The Unpopular President

While he was in office, he was one of the most unpopular presidents to ever serve the United States. He was ridiculed in public print, accused of being power mad, and called a tyrant by one leading newspaper editor of the day. Some said he used the office of President just to gain favor and become rich, and critics didn't even like the parties he gave. On and on it went.

His Secretary of State resigned in disagreement over foreign policy. Two of his Cabinet members quit and formed an opposing political party to fight him. There were riots in the streets, and

congress refused to give him an army to enforce the law. Everyone felt the United States was on the brink of a full-scale civil war. Predictably, scores of newspapers and many American patriots demanded his immediate resignation.

He ultimately declared: "I would rather be in the grave, than in the Presidency."

Sound familiar? No, it is not who you think it is.

This was the man on whom later was conferred the highest honor possible: the undying title, the Father of his country. That's right: George Washington.

Feelings may vanish with vision, and misunderstandings rise to cloud issues, but if God ordained this nation, then it didn't come into existence to fail.

He Ended the War

It takes a long time to heal the wounds of war, especially when that war has divided a country down the middle. And our wounds were deep. Not only was much of the land ravished, but the spirits of the men bore scars as well, deep scars.

But words have a healing power. They can offer new beginnings and the promise of hope. And the President of the United States offered those words to the nation. Although he was a Yankee president, he was born in the South. A man of humble beginnings, he was raised in a log cabin, struggled through poverty, and overcame a limited education to be President. Yet, he offered conciliatory words of optimism, not bitter words demanding vengeance.

The reason for his words—he wanted to treat the Southern states as if they had never been away. He wanted to move on as if there had not been a Civil War at all. Simply put, it was forgiveness and pardon that he had in mind. The occasion chosen for this presidential message was Christmas Day—the perfect day to give new peace and hope, don't you agree?

And what were his words? In part he said, "As President of the United States, I extend pardon, absolute and unconditional, to all who directly or indirectly participated in the late rebellion."

Many opposed these words. Some tried to stop them. But they were spoken anyway.

And who was this president? Sounds like Lincoln?

No.

It was his successor, little-known Andrew Johnson, the President who really ended the Civil War.

John McClean

Bull Run Creek ran through his land. It was a quiet place, as places like this often are. For John McClean farmed the rich bottomland of the river near Manassas Junction, Virginia—as beautiful and peaceful a place as one would ever find. Alas, the times were not quiet though.

South Carolina had seceded from the Union, followed by her ten sister states in the South. Two armies now converged for an initial test of national will, and McClean's land provided marching ground for the Union blue and the Confederate gray. A cannon ball went through his roof. Infantry feet smashed his crops. The

first major battle of the Civil War, known as Bull Run, could have been called the Battle of John McClean's Farm.

So, he moved. He moved far from the noise and strife of war to an extremely quiet section of western Virginia, and the war seemed to pass him by. In fact, it was his fond wish that ballots would replace bullets, and McClean gave himself to a quest for peace.

Finally, when the tide of the Confederacy ran out, the tired troops of Robert E. Lee gave us Richmond and retreated west before the onslaught of a mighty war machine commanded by General Ulysses S. Grant. It was then, on another piece of rich Virginia farmland, John McClean watched the war end and realized his wish for peace.

It was he, the man who observed the war's beginning on his former farm, who witnessed Lee and Grant signing the document of surrender in his new living room, now called Appomattox Courthouse.

Level Ground

The decision of Robert E. Lee to enter West Point was natural for the son of a military family. His graduation as Captain of Cadets earned for him an appointment in the elite Engineering Corps. Tributes to his engineering skill still stand in Ft. Monroe, Virginia, and Charleston Harbor, South Carolina. Yet, it was the Mexican War that was his first testing ground. The American commander Winfield Scott bagged Mexico City, and a Presidential candidacy with it, because a young engineer named Lee found an unguarded approach to the city.

So it was no surprise when he was offered the command of the Union forces in the field at the outset of the Civil War. He turned it down to defend his Virginia.

McClellan, Polk, McClellan again, Burnside, Hooker, they were all Union generals he met and defeated in battle.

Finally, there was Grant, who never really beat him but instead wore him out. After that came Appomattox followed by a time of healing the country's wounds while serving as President of Washington College, later named Washington and Lee University.

But maybe he proved his personal greatness best during a Communion service at the Church of the Presidents in Washington. A black man knelt first. Without hesitation Lee knelt beside him.

When asked why, he said, "Why not? The ground is always level at the foot of the cross."

Get Into the Game

He was an orphan, could run like the wind, and had one great love: baseball. While playing outfield and stealing bases for the Marshalltown, Iowa team, he was noticed by the manager of the Chicago White Sox. Now in the late 19th century that was as close to paradise as any boy who loved baseball could get, to be noticed by the Chicago White Sox. And, while he played for Chicago, he led that team in stealing bases.

Why, one year he stole ninety-five! And the country boy from Marshalltown seemed on his way to making a permanent place for himself in baseball glory.

But it all changed when he met and fell in love with a girl from the Jefferson Park Presbyterian Church. That love led to yet another love, and it sort of took the heart out of baseball for him. Oh, he was still before the crowd, and in one sense still performed, but it was quite different from running down fly balls and stealing bases.

You probably don't know that he appeared before 100 million people in his life, and that was in the days before radio and television. Yet, he always looked like a ball player.

"Take a stand and get into the game!" was one of his slogans.

It is said that he introduced at least a million people into this new kind of life. But it was a different game with a different crowd, and it was for a different cause.

The man who never forgot baseball was the man who played his best game for God— America's greatest revival preacher: outfielder and base-stealer Billy Sunday.

Baby Face

George was born in Baltimore on February 6, 1895. He lived above the saloon his father ran until he was seven. By then he was more of a problem than his folks could handle. He cussed, chewed tobacco, refused to go to school, and ran wild in the streets. Finally, after he stole a dollar from his father's till, he landed in a boys' home for delinquents, and that was where he learned to play baseball.

He signed his first professional contract in 1914 for $600 per year and seventeen years later was drawing $80,000. Someone pointed out that 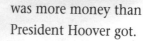 was more money than President Hoover got.

"Well," George replied, "I had a better year than Hoover."

He was one of the smartest men to ever play the game; he seemed to never be out of position or throw to the wrong base. He was also a pitcher of great ability, but we remember him best because of his prodigious hitting. Along the way he picked up a nickname because of his soft features . . . Babe . . . George Herman Babe Ruth.

In addition to his physical skills, he was an incurable optimist. In the World Series of 1932, he pointed toward the center field bleachers and then proceeded to blast the ball out of the park at that very spot.

After the game a sports writer asked, "Babe, what if you missed? What if you failed?"

"You know," Babe said, "I never thought of that."

Take It or Leaf It

When it first got to America, nobody knew what to do with it. Some people buttered and salted the little dried leaves and munched on them as special treats on cold New England nights. Others just boiled it all for an hour or more and drank the bitter, black brew without sugar or milk.

It was said that this plant could raise spirits, soothe nerves, give comfort, and offer cures. As a drink it was refreshing, bracing, calming, and cheering.

It was touted as an aphrodisiac guaranteed to produce "ferocious love bouts" and "lusty desire." To others, it was a miracle liquid said to aid insomnia, asthma, and fertility.

We're not really sure of its origin. It could have come from China or India or Tibet or Burma. But we do know it spread all over Southwest Asia, Africa, Russia, and even South America. When it finally arrived in Europe, medical men called it "pernicious to health." The clergy denounced it as the "demoralizer of the working man."

But the Colonists in our New World finally figured out how they liked it, and the brew became our national beverage. It very likely would have remained that way if the English hadn't decided to tax it. We loved those little leaves so much by then that we were prepared to fight over them.

"Taxation without representation" was our battle cry, and the Revolutionary War was fought, in part at least, because of tea.

The Happy Parasite

It's hard to believe that anything that could bring so much joy is classified as a parasite. But it's true!

The technical name for this Christmas delight is literally "tree thief." Of course it's not all bad. I mean it's good enough that Oklahoma made the decoration its official state flower.

To the early inhabitants of the British Isles, it was a magical plant and the object of worship. Some ancients wore it around the neck to ward off disease. Others stuck a sprig in their hats to guarantee good hunting.

The Japanese were convinced that it would increase crop growth and fertility. The Swiss shot it out of trees with arrows for good luck and happy days.

Italian peasants thought the happy parasite offered protection against harm in general and fire in particular. In old England the first cow that produced a calf after New Year's Day was bedecked with a garland of its leaves.

Our early colonists kept sprigs of the plant under their pillows to induce dreams of happy days to come. Young girls believed they could get a dream-preview of their future spouses.

You know what it is?

Sure you do! You've seen plenty of it every year, even though no one in America today expects it to drive away evil spirits, roll back prices, or solve the energy crisis.

But it does enliven dull parties and offer hope to the kiss-less. It's mistletoe, of course.

The First Westerner

The conquering of the West has become an American symbol, because the movement of our country in that direction has demonstrated over and over again the courage, determination, and free spirit of our people.

One of the first men to explore the area west of the Carolinas was Daniel Boone. He had spent years at a time in the woods, hunting, trapping, camping, and surveying, trying to beat a path into Kentucky. Before he made it, he'd been captured and adopted by an Indian tribe and escaped, seen a brother killed and families massacred, nearly died in a blizzard, and once almost drowned. But he never gave up.

In 1775 he led a small group of about thirty men through the

Cumberland Gap in East Tennessee. From there they cleaned up woodland paths, connected trails beaten down by wandering bison, rolled away rocks, and hacked down forests. They cut through brush and posted guide markers to get through difficult areas. Three hundred miles later, they stopped at the Ohio River where Louisville is today, and that trail became known as the Wilderness Road. Within the next fifteen years, 100,000 people traveled the Wilderness Road to open up the West.

Daniel Boone, the first westerner, may have died penniless. But, his land, his west, shaped and secured the nation that was just being born.

Chimney Tops

Up in the Smokies, there's a mountain called Chimney Tops. Now by Himalayan standards, it's more like a small hill. But it proved to be a fairly strenuous Saturday morning vacation climb for me.

For nearly seven miles I wound around through dense forest, crossing back and forth across a mountain stream, pausing often to sit on broad, cool stones to drink in the silence of the forest and the cool mountain air. There were two peaks on the mountain connected by a ridge. The first peak was still in the forest, and the view from it, for which I had begun the climb much earlier, was still 200 yards away across the ridge.

The gradual upward slope of the ridge took me out past the trees and into the wind. The last few yards to the top were hand over hand up a rock formation with a really frightening drop-off on both sides.

When I got to the top, I sat on the highest rock I could find and looked across the mountains and the valleys, far enough to see where the mountains faded into the horizon and deep enough to see the cars on the highway looking like toys.

Then I looked back across the ridge I had crossed, and saw America, a land of people seeking to climb through the forests and cross the ridges to reach the peaks. I saw a land characterized by people who rise to scale heights and pause to enjoy cool breezes—people who are shaped and taught and helped by the land they live in.

Strawberry Lemonade

During the summer of 1857, the Mabie Circus was making a tour through the South. One of the clowns suddenly decided to leave the troupe. The manager called on Pete Conklin, one of the sideshow barkers, to fill in. Pete did well, so well that he asked for a raise. The manager said he hadn't done that well. Pete, mad, quit.

But he was broke, so he tagged along with the circus as a lemonade-seller. Lemons were scarce and expensive in 1857, so Pete made his lemonade with tartaric acid and sugar.

One hot day, he did such a brisk business that he ran out of his thirst quencher. Rushing to a nearby tent, he picked up the first bucket of water he could find, stirred in some tartaric acid, and was back in business again.

It wasn't until he poured the first glass that he noticed his new lemonade was pink. He couldn't imagine how the color had changed, but with good old-fashioned American ingenuity he made the most of it.

"Strawberry lemonade," he shouted. "Try my new strawberry lemonade." People did; they loved it.

Today there's not a circus anywhere without pink lemonade. And how did Pete Conklin's lemonade get that color?

Well after 119 years I guess it's safe to tell his secret—a performer's red tights had just been soaking in that bucket of water and turned the lemonade pink.

Impossible

It was a company joke that had been tried on every embryonic engineer since the electric light was scarcely a gleam in Edison's eye. The service engineer would be assigned the "impossible" task of frosting electric light bulbs on the inside.

A new engineer at General Electric, Marvin Pipkin, was put through the usual routine. Not being aware that it was a joke, he discovered a way not only to frost bulbs on the inside, but also to etch the glass with soft, rounded pits which gave the bulbs added strength and affected a maximum diffusion of the light.

Fortunately no "wise guy" told Marvin Pipkin that he had been assigned the impossible, so he went ahead and did it.

Edward Weston walked from New York to California, which is 3,895 miles, in 104 days because somebody said he couldn't do it. Then, he turned around and walked back 3,600 miles in seventy-seven days. And he was more than seventy years old.

Pete Gray played Major League Baseball with only one arm.

Florence Chadwick raced in swimming meets for nineteen years and never won once. Coaches called her a misfit and told her to quit. But at thirty-five she was acclaimed the greatest distance swimmer in the world.

All these people had one thing in common; they wouldn't give up.

It's like an old teacher of mine said, "You can't say can't!"

The American Portrait

America, it's easy to paint your portrait in bright, uncomplicated colors—colors like the red, white, and blue of your flag, your hamburger stands, your parades, and your old *Saturday Evening Post* covers; even colors depicting the darkness of your slums, racial problems, and economic inequities. But you're a country of vivid contrasts, of brilliant sun and sudden shadows, of floral print suburbs and harsh montages of industry. And even as the paint dries, the mood changes and your portrait is once more incomplete.

The painter's difficulties are not really surprising. He has to stretch his canvas across 3,615,123 square miles, from the southern tip of Hawaii to the eastern point of Maine. Now, you tell me, where does the painter really find Our Town, Main Street, U.S.A.?

And on what great canvas could he portray fifty quite different states containing nearly 210 million individuals?

How do we paint your portrait? Our palettes are new, our colors are fresh, and our brushes are ready. Then you appear in yet another light, making us realize that once again we've only captured your profile . . . a mere outline of the personality within.

But, we'll keep trying, America, as long as you let us.

She Made the War

Harriet was a P.K. You know: a preacher's kid. Actually you might want to upgrade that a bit to a T.O. (Theologian's offspring) since her father was Lyman Beecher, President of Lane Theological Seminary in Cincinnati, Ohio.

It was there she met and married Calvin Stowe who was a seminary professor.

Harriet was appalled by the slavery that flourished across the Ohio River in Kentucky. Outraged by the passage of the Fugitive Slave Act of 1850, a law that required the return of all runaway slaves, she began writing a novel. It first appeared in serial form in the abolitionist journal, *National Era*.

In 1852 her story was released as a book and sold 350,000

copies the first year. By 1860 it had been translated into twenty languages and produced as a play on countless stages in the United States and abroad.

By dramatizing the plight of slaves through easily understood and highly sympathetic characters, Harriet caught the conscience of the North and brought new respectability to the cause of abolition.

So great was the impact of her book that when President Abraham Lincoln met her he said, "So you're the little woman who wrote the book that made this war."

The book to which Lincoln ascribed this credit was Harriet Beecher Stowe's *Uncle Tom's Cabin*.

The Successful Failure

America is, among other things, the chance to succeed—no matter what. Take this man for instance.

In '31 he failed in business.

He was defeated for the state legislature in '32.

He failed again in business in '33.

In '34 he won his first election—a seat in the state legislature.

But the death of his sweetheart was a severe blow in '35 and led to a nervous breakdown in '36.

And so it was '38 before he was fully recovered, but that was the year of his defeat for speaker of the house.

He attempted to become an elector in the presidential

election of '40 but again was rejected by the voters.

In '43 he ran for a seat in the U.S. Congress and was defeated.

But this was reversed in '46 when he ran again and was elected United States Congressman.

He tried for the U.S. Senate in '58 and lost.

He experienced eleven personal and public defeats in twenty-seven years. But he never quit trying.

And then, in '60, he was elected President of the United States. That's right—1860. And that loser became our 16th President—Abraham Lincoln—perhaps the greatest of them all.

So hang onto this America. The defeats do not count. It's final victory that really matters.

First Lady

Anna was a shy, plain child. Her beautiful mother nicknamed her "Granny" because she was so solemn and serious. Everyone in the family dominated her. Anna had a private tutor and did not go to classes with other children till she was twelve, and at fifteen she went to England to attend a private boarding school for girls.

When her education was finished, she returned to New York where she met Frank. They fell in love and got married. Frank finished law school, and politics seemed to be his future in life till tragedy struck him down in the form of polio.

His dominating mother wanted him to retire and become a country gentleman. But Anna insisted that public service was his place. Frank accepted her support, and one day they walked into the White House together—he as President—she as his first lady.

There she took an energetic interest in national and world affairs. She traveled, gave speeches, and fought for the rights of the poor and oppressed. She wrote a daily newspaper column called "My Day" which greatly increased her popularity.

Since she was born to a wealthy family, it's interesting that Anna became such a champion of the poor. Once a shy, awkward child, she grew into a confident, effective, international stateswoman. Living in a world where women were expected to be decorative and ladylike, she worked at being beautiful in spirit.

She was a great lady, that Anna Eleanor Roosevelt.

The Statue of Liberty

For millions it's been love at first sight. She's taller than the other girls and maybe just a bit heavier. This year she's ninety! And, she's America's favorite lady. Somehow her beauty never diminishes. Rather she's more striking and memorable every time she's seen. And you really can't miss her, I mean, how can you?

She weighs 225 tons and has a 35-foot waist! Her right arm is forty-two feet long with an index finger measuring eight feet. One fingernail weighs 100 pounds! And, by the way, she stands thirty stories tall. She's so precisely constructed  that she sways gently with the breeze, yet built so strongly that she can withstand an 150 mile-an-hour gale.

That's right . . . the Statue of Liberty,
America's favorite lady. She has been the
thrilling first sight of freedom for millions of
new citizens, and the reassuring promise of
liberty for all that claim her.

"Keep, ancient lands, your storied pomp!"
    cries she
With silent lips. "Give me your tired, your
    poor,
Your huddled masses yearning to breathe free.
The wretched refuse of your teeming shore,
Send these, the homeless, tempest-tossed
    to me,
I lift my lamp beside the golden door."

The Friend of Football

He began life as a weak and sickly boy, tortured with asthma. He was timid, afraid, and unlucky. During his teens he broke his arm, his wrist, his nose, his ribs, and his shoulder, and fractured his leg. Yet by sheer willpower and determination, he built himself into a magnificent physical specimen.

He became a noted horseman, went west to be a cowboy, and played a leading part in America's victory in the Spanish-American War. He was an expert rifle shooter, and his marksmanship made him a famous big-game hunter. To overcome his fear of heights, he scaled the Matterhorn. He was an amateur boxer so good that he often sparred with famous fighters. A glancing blow from one of

them during a heated bout cost him the sight of one eye for the rest of his life.

Then, in 1905, when 32 players were killed on football fields, the wrath of the public was aroused. Thirty state legislatures introduced bills to make the sport a crime. He called a conference of College Presidents, and insisted that football was a game worth playing, worth improving, and worth saving. Under his leadership, the National Collegiate Athletic Association was organized.

Football grew and prospered, all because of the efforts of the 26th President of the United States, a man who personally never played the game or even liked it.

Teddy Roosevelt was a friend of football.

Thanks for New York City

Peter Minuet is part of America, even if his position with the West India Trading Company doesn't leave you breathless. It was a growing company, but he was only the third in a line of directors. Nonetheless, he put together one of the biggest bargain packages in real estate history.

It's true that Thomas Jefferson bought more acreage for us in the famous Louisiana Purchase, and our Civil War Secretary of State Seward surely picked up more natural resources when he paid for Alaska.

But it's really hard to beat Peter Minuet's purchase in ultimate value. The real estate deal was settled on May 24, 1626, in the presence of local

Indians and some Dutch colonists who lived in bark-covered huts in a colony called Ft. Amsterdam. On that day, Peter Minuet gave sixty gilders to his Indian landlords for an island. Actually it was a peninsula he bought, not an island. But that never really mattered to Peter. He simply wanted a place where the Dutch could trade and farm and grow. He wanted a place they could call their own.

And he had a vision for a colony of hundreds, perhaps even thousands. Sixty gilders: that's about twenty-four dollars in today's money. Not a bad price for an island, not at all when you remember that we're talking about Manhattan Island.

Thank you, Peter, for giving us New York City.

Helping Hands

Her father was taken as a prisoner of war when the Union Army captured Savannah in 1864, and the incident had a profound effect on five-year-old Juliette.

She came to know how it felt to go without things; so after her daddy came home she organized a group of neighborhood girls to help relieve the serious clothing shortage. They called themselves, "The Helping Hands."

The first thing they tried to make was a jacket. They held it up to Julie's brother and it fell to pieces. The boys on the block quickly changed the name to "Helpless Hands."

But Julie was undaunted. She was sure there was something she could do. She

worked to improve her skills and traveled to learn new crafts.

Forty-six years later she gathered together another group of girls. It was 1912, again in Savannah, Georgia, when she invited young ladies to learn to sew, cook, weave, and even raise chickens. She talked glowingly of camping trips and cooking contests. She ignored the critics who said most of what she proposed was "unladylike," and soon there were hundreds of groups modeled after hers and thousands of members.

She didn't call them "Helping Hands" anymore. She changed the name, and her young ladies continue to spread the spirit of sisterhood and sharing.

Juliette Gordon Low gave us the Girl Scouts.

We Were Broke

Beyond the trenches, the allied armies formed two long lines: the French on one side, the Americans on the other. At one o'clock the British marched out. Every one of them kept his eyes riveted on the French troops, as if trying to blot out those Colonials on the other side of the road.

Marquis de Lafayette snapped an order, and the American band exploded with "Yankee Doodle." As if on a string, every British head was jerked around by the sound, and they stared, unwillingly, into the eyes of their ex-subjects.

"Done in the trenches before Yorktown in Virginia, October 19, 1781."

The British had surrendered!

One of Washington's aides, Tench Tilghman, was given the

honor of carrying the victory report to the Continental Congress in Philadelphia, and I suppose the story of his trip is the best possible illustration of the narrow margin between American victory and defeat.

When Tilghman arrived, he asked Congress to give him a draft of money to pay for the expenses of his journey.

They couldn't do it!

There was not one cent left in the National Treasury so each Congressman contributed a dollar out of his own pocket.

One Vote

The prisoner was a woman, unusual in 19th century America. And the fine was large for that day—$100.00 plus court costs.

After being held for some time in a New York jail, the prisoner finally had her day in court. It was a brief day as lawyers for the defense and the state presented their cases quickly. The verdict was equally fast in coming; she was guilty as charged. Anyone could understand that.

There followed the sentencing, and it seemed all over. But almost as an afterthought, and possibly out of courtesy to his unusual

woman prisoner, the judge asked if she wished to speak. She stood tall and erect in the prisoners' dock.

"Yes, your honor," she said.

"I do have something to say. In your judgment of guilty, you have trampled underfoot every principle of government and ignored my rights as a citizen. I am degraded, as is all my sex, by Your Honor's verdict today."

When she sat down, it was somehow different. She never paid that fine. And her release from custody came that same day. Beyond this, she dramatized the cause fifty years before its triumph.

Her crime?

Susan Anthony had presented herself at the Rochester, New York, polls and had voted in a presidential election. And things were never the same after that one courageous lady stood up to be counted.

Presidents

It wasn't until seven days before he was inaugurated that the people decided what to call George Washington. Originally the official title was to be "His Highness, the President of the United States, and Protector of the Liberty." But on April 23rd, 1789, the Senate decided to designate him simply "The President."

Now most of us are inclined to believe that all presidents are intellectual giants, men of great stature and accomplishment. But that's hardly true. Take Zachary Taylor for example. Before he was elected, he had never voted in his life—not even once! When they asked him if he

was a Whig or a Democrat, he said he didn't rightly know. When the Whigs nominated him anyway and notified him by mail, he refused to pay the ten cents postage due and sent the nomination back, unopened.

And how about William Henry Harrison and how he came to be president? He was nominated because he had "no ideas" which could either interest or infuriate anybody. In a sad exclamation point to his nonimpact on history, he caught cold during his own Inaugural Address and died thirty days later.

Or John Tyler, who couldn't get a job after he left office. He finally went to work at a village pound where he tended stray horses and cows.

How about Van Buren who was so vain that when they auctioned off his White House goods, the carpet was threadbare in front of the mirror where he'd practiced his speeches.

And these were our leaders.

No wonder we say, "In God we trust."

Naismith's Game

James Naismith was a physical education instructor at the international YMCA training school in Springfield, Massachusetts, when the winter of 1891 proved to be an exceptionally cold one—so cold that outdoor sports were out of the question, and the young men were getting tired of the routine calisthenics.

James' superior, Luther Gulick, head of the physical education staff, asked him to try and devise a game that could be played indoors on winter evenings. He challenged him to create something that would be challenging and competitive as well as demanding physically.

That was a big order for a thirty-year-old beginning instructor. But Naismith took it seriously and went to work on the project. He devised a fast-moving, minimum contact game with the ball controlled by the hands only.

He tacked two old peach containers on the gymnasium balcony and divided his students into two teams. Each team had nine men. They played with a soccer ball, and the game seemed to catch on quickly as others picked up the new Naismith game.

Two years later with certain refinements and player changes, Geneva College and the University of Iowa played the new indoor game, and Americans have been playing it ever since.

James Naismith, in trying to come up with an indoor team sport where a group of players could work out and enjoy it, had discovered a new athletic creation—the only truly American sport—basketball.

Not Needed

The patent was taken out following a year of paperwork, preparing for a demonstration of the new device. The date was June 1, 1869, and the patented device was oddly modern. It was an electrical vote recorder that would permit a vote taken by a congressional body to be counted and announced instantly.

The inventor, though unknown, was a young man of promise and skill. The device was demonstrated in Washington and proved totally successful. Think what this would mean in time conservation, speeding up the process of necessary legislation, and giving Congressmen more time for essential committee work.

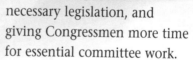

The hopeful inventor was filled with optimism, only to

hear the congressional committee chairman report the following decision regarding the new vote recorder: "Young man, if there is any invention on earth that we don't want, it is this one."

The Congressional feeling was that it would add too much speed to debate, and thus endanger the test of time needed to make right decisions.

Another kind of man might have given up, but not this one. He had the right idea, just ahead of his time. Turning his inventive genius to more current needs, the rejected inventor began a series of successful work that lasted a lifetime.

The man whose first try ended in public failure became the most productive inventor of America: Thomas Alva Edison.

Copy Cat

Chester Carlson had an idea. As a patent lawyer he dreaded all the copy work required in reproducing detailed drawings and descriptions. He wanted some kind of machine where you could just "push a button and get a copy." Since no one had a better idea, he started to work on his.

Fifteen years passed by from his project's beginning till the first piece of commercial equipment went on the market. And for ten of those years he worked on his own limited resources, conducting his research in a tiny room behind a beauty parlor in New York.

Carlson made his breakthrough on October 22, 1938. The first message ever duplicated by the process was simply the date and place: "10-22-38 ASTORIA." The copy was produced by the action of an electrically charged surface that was treated with a resinous powder.

At least twenty companies rejected the invention. But in 1944 the Battelle Memorial Institute of Columbus, Ohio, finally invested in the machine, and in Detroit on October 22, 1948, exactly ten years to the day from when the first copy was produced, Chester Carlson staged his first public demonstration.

"I'm happy with the way it all worked out," he said, "but sometimes I got a little impatient."

But we'll all agree, Chester, the XEROX copy machine was worth the wait.

He Never
Won a Battle

If you could ask George Washington to name his profession, he probably would say farmer-soldier, in that order. You see, when his fellow countrymen sought him in 1775 to lead a Continental army against England, it was really the call of expediency. Very few patriots had ever commanded the troops in battle. Washington had, and thus the job sought him.

His army was a disappointment. A rag-tag group of thirteen armies meeting together, each loyal to its own state and uncertain about a common cause. One disaster followed another.

The battle of Brooklyn ended en route. Then Ft. Washington and Ft. Lee were lost. At Monmouth, subordinance failed, and the battle was

scarcely saved by Washington riding in himself. In fact, Washington's intervention turned out to produce only a draw. Trenton's successful surprise attack was not really a battle as much as a predawn takeover. Then there was Valley Forge in winter, New Jersey, and more defeats. Next came three long years of waiting while the war moved south.

It was finally at Yorktown that the decisive victory came with the surrender of the British general Cornwallis. But even there Washington's army came late to a British force already bottled up by the French.

No. George Washington may not have won the individual battles—but he proved that, through perseverance, you can still win the war.

No Room

The man rode proudly up to the largest hotel in Baltimore, entered the crowded lobby, and asked for a room. The landlord, a man named Boyden, surveyed the guest's appearance and assumed him to be a farmer. Feeling he would not be a fitting guest to his fine hotel, Boyden said, "We have no room for you, Sir."

The farmer turned around, called for his horse, and departed. It was then that someone got the courage to tell the landlord that he had turned away the greatest man alive, the Vice President of the United States.

After Boyden recovered from his shock, he gathered his servants together and sent them to bring the gentleman back. "Tell him he may have forty rooms if he wishes. Tell him to please come back. He can have my own room if he wants it. What have I done? He shall have the best of everything!"

Meanwhile, the Vice President had run into some old friends. They were all staying at the Globe Hotel, and he joined them for food and reminiscence. It was there that the landlord's servants found him and relayed their master's message.

The Vice President listened—then replied, "Tell Mr. Boyden that I have engaged a room and am very pleased here. I appreciate his good intentions, but if he has no room for a dirt-farmer, he has no room for Thomas Jefferson—for we are alike and the same!"

Valley Forge

It was at Valley Forge, almost 200 years ago, that the people of the United States proved that they had the courage to be a nation. Valley Forge is known as one of America's finest hours, but the only battle ever fought there was the battle of hunger and cold and despair.

You see the plains of Valley Forge and Pennsylvania were the last citadels of a dissipated American army. After two disastrous defeats at the hands of the British, General George Washington had led his discouraged troops in retreat to Valley Forge for the winter.

The winds blew across the plains, and temperatures dropped far below zero in one of the worst winters in history. The General himself wrote,

"There are men in camp unfit for duty, because they are barefoot and naked."

The soldiers lived in small huts built of logs and clay. Many sat up all night by the fire because there were not enough blankets. There was near famine in the camp; men went for weeks without meat. But Washington provided strict discipline for strength, and his wife Martha tempered it with tenderness as she moved among the men daily, praying for them.

When spring arrived they took count. One-third of the army had died and another third of the army had quit and gone home. The remaining third simply marched out and won the Revolutionary War.

The United States of America was born.

Big Enough

It began officially when President Calvin
Coolidge placed a drill in the hands of a
workman in South Dakota. But it really started
long before that in the heart and mind of an
Idaho-born patriot, Gutzon Borglum, who was
primarily a man with a mission, a sculptor
seeking something big enough to fashion in
honor of his country.

"There is not one monument big enough for
America," he would often say. But Borglum found
his challenge in the Black Hills of South Dakota.

The southeastern face of a
5,700-foot granite mountain
suggested a monumental
sculpture in honor of his
country. It would be the
resolute Washington, the

visionary Jefferson, the deep wisdom of Lincoln, and the vigor of Teddy Roosevelt, all done massively in 60-foot faces.

Nine times Borglum remade his model. He climbed scaffolds; he trained others; he checked everything, even the effect of a shadow on a cheek or chin. Gutzon Borglum carved and chipped through fourteen summers, but he died seven months before the project was finished. His son completed his work.

Today a million tourists a year see Borglum's monument that's big enough for America. And you know, in a way we're all sculptors. Borglum left behind Mt. Rushmore. What will you leave?

The Unusual Coach

He was a frail lad with weak eyes. He had to wear glasses all of his life, and he hated them. Those spectacles were a constant reminder of his poor vision and how it kept him from his first love, baseball. But he soon learned that even though he couldn't play, he could organize and coach.

So he led his local team to a winning season. Later when he attended Princeton, he tried again to be a baseball player. But failing to make the varsity, he turned once more to managing. After graduation he returned to Princeton and became the football coach. He was considered a top strategist and gridiron wizard. In fact, he changed the whole concept of football coaching.

He was the first coach to work out plays and formations by using charts and graphs. But as well as being innovative, he was also one of the most unusual football coaches of all time. He never blustered or ranted or gave his players "do or die" talks. Instead, he lectured on honor, decency, cooperation, and sportsmanship. By his leadership, this soft-spoken man produced a mighty Princeton eleven that compiled an awesome record of gridiron victories.

Not only did such tactics of leadership carry his team upward, they made Woodrow Wilson, the 28th president of the United States, one of the most beloved peacemakers who ever lived.

The Ticket Taker

When Stanford University opened its doors in 1891, he was one of the first to enroll. He wanted to play football, but Stanford had no team, so he tried baseball. It was shortstop that he wanted to play, but he wasn't good enough, so they made him ticket taker. There were no grandstands and no fences so he had to chase down and take twenty-five cents from anybody who got close.

He collected dollars, one quarter at a time, until one day there was enough to start putting together the football team of which he had dreamed. He scrounged for equipment, buying secondhand gear and one football. He tried to play; it was still no use. He wasn't even good enough to make it on his own team.

But he kept working for his dream. He sold tickets, ushered people to their seats, helped the players dress, and gave pep talks to start them off.

Then he signed a contract to play the University of California. The idea was absurd. The ragamuffin Stanford squad had no chance against the mightiest team in the West. Well, 27,000 spectators turned out anyway, and they got the shock of their lives.

Stanford won!

I mean they beat California in the greatest upset in the history of football, all because he believed.

When he couldn't do what he wanted to, he did what he could. I suppose that it was that self-sacrificing devotion to duty that started Herbert Hoover on his way to becoming the 31st President of the United States.

Cup of Cold Water

Ted and Dorothy Hustad settled in Wall, South Dakota, because they liked the challenge of an undiscovered place. There were friendly people and great amounts of room to grow, so they opened a drugstore. But those early days were difficult.

Customers were few and far between. Somehow a specialty was needed, some service that would be unique, some extra expression of care. One hot summer Ted and Dorothy hit upon an idea—free ice water. At first it sounded silly, but they put the first sign up on the major road leading into town: "Free Ice Water at Walls Drug Store."

Some people did come, and that led to another sign on the opposite side of town. Business

picked up. Ted and Dorothy kept putting up signs until every South Dakota highway had at least one "Ice Water" sign from Walls Drugstore. It was catching on, and so was their business. Somehow a cup of cold water given in the South Dakota heat was cooling the bodies and warming the hearts of weary travelers.

And, what about today?

Well, you can find a sign at the Taj Mahal in India which reads: "Free Ice Water at Walls Drugstore, 10,728 Miles, Wall, South Dakota." And back at the store, 6,000 people every week visit Ted and Dorothy Hustad, all because of a cup of cold water.

The Real Dixie

In 1859 Daniel Emmett, a New York minstrel man, wrote a song based on words and music he had once heard slaves singing in the Carolinas about a happy place called "Dixieland." Emmett's parody of their song was an instant success, and during the Civil War it became the official anthem of the Confederacy.

But what Dan Emmett never knew was that "Dixieland" was not in the South—but actually had been right in New York, just a few miles from where he wrote his famous song.

While the Dutch still ruled Manhattan, one of the pioneers decided that he might grow tobacco on the island so he brought in some slaves from

Africa. When his farm failed, he sent his workers to a plantation in South Carolina.

It was there that the word "Dixieland" was first used in song. For you see, the Dutch farmer who owned the slaves in Manhattan had been a generous man, and the slaves wished they could be back on his farm. They sang "I wish I was in Dixieland" because the name of that kind Dutch farmer was Johaan Dixie.

A Dime Will Do

Frank started out slowly. No one really knew what he had in him. He was born on a New York farm in 1852. He had a limited but adequate education, including two short terms in a small business college, before going to work as a clerk in a dry goods store.

Frank stayed at that long enough to know he didn't care to work for other people—he wanted to do his own thing. He had ideas and dreams that just didn't fit the mold of established business practices.

So in 1879, in Lancaster, Pennsylvania, he opened his first store. Things went well, and he expanded. He opened another store—then two more.

But it was too fast, and three of his first shops failed.

But Frank was sure that his primary rule of mass merchandising would succeed—volume sale of low-priced goods, attractively displayed—at a modest profit. Nothing in his stores sold for more than ten cents.

And he was right. People did respond to his dream, and his chain grew until by 1919, when Frank died, he owned 1,000 stores. And in New York City in 1913, his company built a skyscraper that for years was the world's tallest—named in his honor—the man who gave us the "Dime-Store"—Frank Winfield Woolworth.

The Borrowed Name

Bill hated to write. Oh, he loved to put stories together in his head. It was the task of putting them down on paper that wasn't worth his time. When he did write, he was probably trying to forget, pushing the past out of mind.

You see, once upon a time Bill had worked for a bank. And when he heard a shortage had been detected in his accounts, he took off for Central America. When he returned, he found his wife had died in his absence—of grief and tuberculosis. So he gave himself up, and Bill Porter went to prison for five years. It was there that he began to write. And write he did—250 short stories in the next seven years.

"Rule one" he would say, "is to write stories that please yourself. There is no rule two."

His stories never sold for much—twenty, thirty, sometimes a hundred dollars. One was made into a Broadway play. The producer got $100,000. Bill got practically nothing.

But he kept writing using his special formula. He used to say that sometimes he wrote the ending first and then wrote a story to fit it.

Whatever he did, he produced classics with the surprise endings that came to be called by his name. Not Bill Porter, but an adopted name—you could say a real "pen name," because he borrowed it from the captain of the Penitentiary guards, Henry, O. Henry.

The Chirographer

There are some things a nice girl doesn't do, even if they're legal. One hundred years ago, most of America was still frontier, and when Christopher Sholes invented a ladies' sized chirographer, he couldn't get any sales. It just wasn't ladylike. In an effort to dignify the practice, he got the YWCA in New York to offer free courses in the care and use of the chirographer. It was no use; it was good, but not nice.

Even after Christopher Sholes got the most famous gunsmith in America to manufacture it for him, he only sold 1,200 in seven years. But in 1875 the gunsmith received a letter, and everything changed. A man said he had one around his house and found it efficient, but, and

these are his exact words, "I don't want people to know that I own this little joker."

The letter was signed, Samuel Clemens . . . you know, Mark Twain. Now a secret like that was just too good to keep, and word got around fast. By now millions are in daily use. Ladies using them have become expert enough to make a profession of it.

The chirographer that Mark Twain and the Remington Gun Company told the world about went on to write its own place in history. You see, the chirographer was the earliest name for an American dream come true: the typewriter.

Watch the Birdy

George became fatherless when he was fourteen, and to support his mother and two sisters, he worked as a bank clerk. He never did have much money, but he had a wealth of determination.

Along the way, he picked up interest in a new "hobby." He became quite proficient in all its processes. George kept working days at the bank, but he spent every evening for three years experimenting in his mother's kitchen on what he called a dry gelatin. Eventually he came up with a paper that could carry his dry emulsion.

He decided to make it available to the general public. He began producing a small box with one roll of his "dry emulsion paper," good for 100

uses. He coined a slogan, "You press the button; we do the rest."

By the early 1900s every national magazine carried colored ads showing charming ladies, sophisticated men, and even children carrying and operating George's little push-button box.

And that box made him rich but never selfish. He donated one hundred million dollars to medical and scientific institutions as well as to education and art.

He died in 1932, and it's strange that there are almost no photographs of George Eastman, the man who turned his simple little box called Kodak into the instrument that revolutionized photography.

Tomorrow

It was in the early 1930s that Los Angeles built her coliseum. Erected for the Olympic games in 1932 with seating capacity of 100,000 plus, she still hosts the University of Southern California and its crosstown rival, the University of California at Los Angeles, as well as a visiting Billy Graham or a fireworks show on the Fourth of July.

But its original intent was Olympic. And 1932 was the year of America's great relay team, four men favored to capture a gold medal. The day of the race, crowds filled the coliseum. The starting gun brought them to their feet. The American was in front. The baton went smoothly to the second man, and he then put more distance between himself

and his nearest competitor. The crowd was wild. But it was at the third lap that it happened.

The exchange was a failure—the baton was dropped. Trying to retrieve it, the third runner broke stride and fell, and the other runners swept by him. There was a defeat in the coliseum that day, but there was a lesson as well. The efforts of two fine runners were canceled by the failure of a third. And the fourth man never had a chance.

America is many generations. No one generation can isolate itself from past or future, and when one generation fails, all that's gone before hurts. And much worse, someone in the tomorrow may never have a chance to run.

The General's Game

Abner Doubleday fired that first Union shot of the Civil War while serving at Fort Sumter in South Carolina's Charleston Harbor. At one time, in the decisive battle of Gettysburg, he commanded all the Northern troops on the field. By the end of the war he was a Major General. After his retirement from the Army he worked for the city of San Francisco. There he turned up an idea for getting trolley cars up and down the steep hills. He called it the Cable Car.

Civil War General, City Engineer, inventor—that's a lot for one life. There's more though. For  we remember him best for something that happened when he was a young West Pointer home on vacation in Cooperstown, New York.

He was training to be an engineer in the Army, and his mind was orderly. So, the confused and haphazard way ball games were played bothered his systematic thought processes. It was only natural that he use his West Point vacation that spring of 1839 to establish a simple, uniform set of rules for a game of ball.

They were first used all over New York. Then during the Civil War, because of the boredom of men in army camps, the game caught on, using Doubleday rules. And, as you know, we still play by them today.

For you see, General Abner Doubleday made his greatest contribution as a twenty-year-old student when he gave us our great American pastime of baseball.

Want to Play

In 1933 the times were hard for most Americans. Charles Darrow was no different. He was an unemployed heating engineer, forty-two years old with a wife and family to care for.

Charles started inventing things to stay occupied. He came up with some game score pads, jigsaw puzzles, and a combination ball and bat beach toy. But none of those ideas proved profitable.

Then Darrow came up with a real estate game as a family diversion for empty evenings. A round piece of oilcloth colored with free paint samples made the playing board. He drew some

funny money, cut up shoeboxes for title deeds to property, and used colored buttons for playing pieces.

Friends began requesting copies after spending an evening around the oilcloth, and soon he was turning out two homemade sets a day. In 1934 he took his idea to Parker Brothers, the world's largest producer of games, but they turned him down. It seems that Charles broke fifty-two Golden Rules for successful games.

Darrow returned home to Pennsylvania and had 5,000 sets made, and by Christmas stores were ordering so many that he was working fourteen hours a day to keep up. Parker Brothers watched the sales and reconsidered in 1935.

And now Charles Darrow's game is the most popular in the world; it is published in fifteen languages. MONOPOLY came to be just because a dad wanted something for his children to do with their evenings.

Pounds for Knowledge

James Smithson was a wealthy British scientist who was regarded as one of the foremost chemists and mineralogists of the nineteenth century. He had amassed a sizable fortune in Great Britain, and he wanted to assist America with research and knowledge.

In 1838 he sent the clipper "Mediator" to Philadelphia with an extraordinary cargo of 104,960 British pounds in gold sovereigns. They arrived in September and were recoined into U.S. money at the Philadelphia mint. But it took our Congress until 1846 to accept his gift of more

than half a million dollars because we weren't sure how to use his specific bequest that was for the foundation of "an establishment for the increase and diffusion of knowledge among men."

Today our institute of science, technology, history, and art is the most important archive of human knowledge, achievement, and culture in the world. More than a museum and laboratory, the institute is involved in performing arts, scientific expeditions, and publishing.

Some twenty million visitors each year walk through the halls named for the great benefactor who sent his gold across the Atlantic but never visited here himself. It was James Smithson who gave us the famous Smithsonian Institute.

Rule of Gold

James was born in Hamilton, Missouri. He was one of twelve children raised in poverty on a farm. His father worked the land six days a week and on Sunday preached in a small church for no pay.

James got his first job in a general store and saved enough money to finally purchase his own butcher shop. To retain the town's leading hotel as a customer, he was expected to buy a bottle of liquor for the head cook each week. But James didn't smoke or drink, and he wouldn't bribe the cook so the hotel didn't buy its meat from his shop.

His butcher business failed.

Later in life he often said, "I lost everything I had, but I learned never to compromise."

His real career began when in Kemmerer, Wyoming, he opened the "Golden Rule" store. Those were the days when everyone bought on credit and paid high prices. He tried a different formula: cash and lower prices to attract more sales. It worked.

He changed the name of his stores as he expanded, but the Golden Rule was still his motto, and by 1927 he had 750 retail stores in forty-five states. Managers were allowed to buy an interest in their stores, and profits were shared with employees.

James believed that Christian ethics and hard work would succeed in business. And, he left 1,700 stores scattered all across America with his name on the front door to prove it: J. C. Penney.

Strength Enough

George was so plagued by illness throughout his life that he was once officially reprimanded for being away from his military duties so often. During his lifetime he suffered from smallpox, pneumonia, malaria, pleurisy, dysentery, rheumatism, and influenza plus back pains, dental problems, and recurring fevers.

In fact, by the time he was twenty-nine George had survived four serious illnesses, any one of which could have proven fatal. He was a big man and possessed incredible physical strength, and that probably kept him alive.

In 1757 during the French and Indian War, he came down with such a severe case of dysentery that he had to leave his troops and spend four months convalescing at home. That's when the Governor of Virginia reprimanded him for being absent from his military duties.

Fortunately, his health was stable through the Revolutionary War except for one illness that occurred in the winter of '77. He suffered an attack of malaria and pneumonia and was so sick he considered turning over his command to General Nathan Greene, but he held on and was a significant factor in the victory of the colonies.

Ironically in 1799 he came down with a sore throat and died. But that man who was plagued by sickness did have strength enough to become the father of our country: George Washington.

A Walk in the Woods

"I might have become a millionaire," he once said, "but I chose to be a tramp."

He was supposed to go into business, marry, and settle down. Instead, at twenty-five, John Muir started wandering. He never called it that. He said he wanted to experience the wilderness; preserve it for others.

That first trip of his never really ended. All his life John Muir kept walking. He roamed the Sierras in the West, as well as the pine and hardwood forests of the Great Lakes, making notes all the time, recording, as he said, "the heart of the world." One hike took him a thousand miles from Indiana to the Gulf of Mexico. Oh, he stopped to work at times, taking a job just long

enough to pick up enough money to send him back to his wilderness.

Then, in the 1870s, loggers began to move into his precious forests, and ranchers began to claim the valleys. Muir realized there would be little wilderness left if something were not done. So he started writing, lecturing, persuading anyone who'd listen to save his wilderness. His triumphs were many, including the Yosemite and Sequoia National Parks, the Petrified Forest, portions of the Grand Canyon, the National Park Service, and the Bureau of Forestry. They're all fruits of his work.

The next time you enjoy nature, remember gratefully the man who went out for a walk in the woods and stayed all his life.

The Forty Mile Wire

"What hath God wrought!" These four words form one of the most significant sentences in our nation's history. And while they speak of God at work, they were not the words of a minister or a theologian. Rather than a pulpit, these words of praise to God were sent from the chambers of the Supreme Court in Washington, D.C., on May 24, 1844.

The man who sent them had been an artist—a portrait painter. But he gave that up to follow another idea. And, that new idea took him to a bleak factory room of the Speedwell Ironworks at Morristown, New Jersey, where he worked mostly with a strange wire—a wire that he believed could change the face of America.

From the Ironworks he moved to a basement room in New York University, and there he strung one mile of his dream wire around and around that limited basement for an experimental test of his idea. And it worked!

Congress appropriated enough money for forty miles of the same wire, enough to reach from Washington, D.C., to Baltimore, Maryland. It was in this setting that the now-famous message "What hath God wrought!" was given.

The idea? Electrical impulses could be sent from point to point.

The event? The first instant communication between cities.

The man? Samuel Findlay Morse, who gave us the Morse Code and his wire—the telegraph line.

Your Place

The people who love this country are the ones who reflect the American ideal of belonging, and a significant part of being American is finding your place, your home, your ground. Americans retain a kind of fascination for their place, a fascination that is stronger than most would ever realize.

A town clerk in a small New England village once wrote: "I've never seen anyone yet who was born or lived in Vermont but who cherished the idea of returning. Because, uh, well," he stammered, "you can't find this in many places. And it's getting more noticeable as time goes on."

In the bustling metropolis of San Francisco, somebody once said about his town, "Everyone

should be allowed to love two cities: his own and San Francisco."

The first people came to America to find their own place. And we of this later age have proven to be no different. You see, in each man everywhere there is that longing to have a place to belong to. And our country has given us an unlimited choice as to where we can choose to settle down. If you look carefully, you can trace this search throughout our history. See it: the pilgrims, the settlers, the cowboys, all searching for a place to call home.

America lends herself to that discovery when each of us finds that particular spot on the map that becomes our place.

The Father Who Cared

Did you know that a man became President of the United States because his son was a poor student? That's right! It all started when Robert tried to get into Harvard back in '59. He had come east from Illinois to take the entrance exams and failed in fifteen subjects.

That worried Dad. Like all fathers, he wanted his son to make good grades and get a fine education. So Dad made a fast trip east to bolster Robert's morale and help tutor him in another bid to gain entrance into Harvard.

While he was there, Dad was invited to have  dinner with a famous editor. That editor was so impressed that he arranged for Dad to give a lecture in New York City.

It was a good speech. His folksy, casual delivery went over big with the New Yorkers. As a result of that one speech, Dad became an overnight sensation.

He was thrust into the national political picture and became a prime candidate for the Republican presidential nomination, which he accepted. Then, he became President of the United States—all because he cared about his son, Robert, who buckled down to his studies and became a fine student.

What was the name of the editor who launched the presidential career? Horace Greeley.

And, the father who became President because his son was a poor student is one of the greatest of all time: Abraham Lincoln.

Remember Franklin

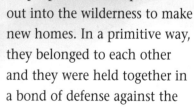

Alaska is the largest, Rhode Island the smallest. California has the most people, and New York is not far behind. All of these we recognize with ease as different states of our Union. Many school children recite all fifty without much trouble. But have you ever heard of Franklin? No, I don't mean the man's name. I mean the state. It is unrecognized and unofficial; still, from a practical aspect, it is an important part of the great family of American states.

Franklin's original land charter was in western North Carolina. The people there had pushed

out into the wilderness to make new homes. In a primitive way, they belonged to each other and they were held together in a bond of defense against the wild land. With a fierce independence, they clamored for separate identity. They wanted their own state.

On August 23, 1784, the men of the west river country met at Jonesboro, North Carolina, and proclaimed the state of Franklin. John Seaver was elected governor.

Well, no one contested their try for statehood; many simply ignored it. That wasn't the reason for us not having a state of Franklin. The real problem was that they simply did not have enough money or manpower, and in four short years it was all over. The little brother state was lost.

It quietly returned home to North Carolina. Now, it's only a memory. But they tried, and for that we owe them. You see, in large part, America is the chance to try, even at the risk of failure.

Lincoln's Best Vote

Every vote means something. This was really the case in 1864. Lincoln was in deep political trouble. The war was dragging into its third unpopular year. In the North, it was becoming "Mr. Lincoln's War," and that opened the door to real doubt as to his reelection.

For the weary people in the North, a new president was the easy way to get out of an endless conflict. To the people in the South, the only chance for a negotiated peace seemed to be a new occupant in the White House. But battlefield successes intervened and insured the President's reelection. Nevertheless, while he won a strong victory, it was not overwhelming.

Lincoln's only known landslide victory was far from

Washington, D.C. No one ever officially announced the total results of the voting even though every ballot was carefully marked, collected, and counted. The final outcome of this one landslide was interesting—even stunning. In it Lincoln received 7,000 votes out of a total of 7,350. That's more than 95 percent—unheard of in popular voting!

The reason for this immense personal popularity? A hometown section in Illinois or a block of elderly people told how to vote? No! The polling place was a "Prisoner of War" Camp at Andersonville, Georgia. And the voters were the captive Union soldiers who believed in their man!

God Bless America

by Irving Berlin

"While the storm clouds gather far across the sea,
Let us swear allegiance to a land that's free,
Let us all be grateful for a land so fair,
As we raise our voices in a solemn prayer.

God Bless America.
Land that I love
Stand beside her, and guide her
Thru the night with a light from above.
From the mountains, to the prairies,
To the oceans, white with foam
God bless America
My home sweet home."

Prayer for America

Our Father:

We thank You for Your bountiful blessings upon this land. For it is Your touch that produces the rich wheat harvests, the more than ample citrus crops, the vast sections of farmland clothed in verdant green, and so much more.

We are humbled when we remember the courage and faith of our founding generations, and we ask for strength that we might carry on the traditions they established. For it was their faith in You that made it possible for our dreams to come true.

We stand in awe when we gaze upon Your majesties: brilliant stars, clear and cold upon the prairies; dewy mornings, quiet in the forest; snow-capped mountains with clear, cold streams;

and the shining sea with its endless mutterings. Your creation remains the ultimate masterpiece.

We become more aware of our place in the grand scheme of Your universe whenever we take the time to look around at the grandeur of America. For it is only when we acknowledge You as the Master Creator of the Universe that we can truly appreciate Your special love for America.

And when we do, when we really, really do see with crystal clarity how blessed America has been and is, then we cannot help but experience anew *The Wonder of America*.

Father, thank You for Your touch. Please never remove it from us, and please keep us aware of our need for it.

Amen.

This is what the LORD says:
"Stand at the crossroads and look;
ask for the ancient paths,
ask where the good way is,
and walk in it, and you will
find rest for your souls."

Jeremiah 6:16 NIV

About the Author

Derric Johnson epitomizes creativity and is renowned for excellent talent and his achievements as a motivational speaker, ordained pastor, prolific songwriter, musician, creative consultant, and author. Derric brings life and artistic genius to everything he does. He is a Stanley Foundation lecturer, featured nationally and internationally. Over the past 20 years, he has served 18 years as a minister; authored 4 books; written 150 original songs, 23 cantatas, and 2,800 musical arrangements; published 32 books of choral collections, with involvement in the production of 94 recorded albums on 12 labels.

He founded and directed The Regeneration, a touring ensemble of singers who traveled more than 1 million miles in 12 years, performing to more than 12 million people in 6,000 concerts.

Derric has been a specialty writer for Radio City Music Hall. For the past 20 years, he has served as a Creative Consultant for Walt Disney World, where he currently is arranging, producing, and staffing EPCOT Center's, The Voices of Liberty.

For additional information on seminars, consulting services, scheduling speaking engagements, or to write the author, please address your correspondence to:

Derric Johnson
P.O. Box 944
Sherwood, Oregon 97140
Or call 1-503-625-1539

Additional copies of this book
are available from your local bookstore.

Also by Derric Johnson:

The Wonder of Christmas

If you have enjoyed this book, or if it has
impacted your life, we would like to hear from you.

Please contact us at:

Honor Books
Department E
P.O. Box 55388
Tulsa, Oklahoma 74137

Or by e-mail at info@honorbooks.com